STANDARD LOAN

Renew Books on PHONE-it: 01443 654456

Books are to be returned on or before the last date below

6/6/10

Cardiff Learning Resources Centre
University of Glamorgan

PLASTIC DESIGN

daab

Introduction 4

During the past 50 years, the plastic industry has grown at an incredible pace until becoming part of nearly all the areas of human activity, including of course architecture, and easily rivaling the steel and iron industry. The word plastic, which comes from the Greek *plastikos* (which means easy to mould) is an organic polymer material, rarely natural (rubber and wax) and frequently synthetic or semi-synthetic, created by large macromolecular chains which contain carbon. It is also inexpensive, flexible, moldable, impermeable, insulating and resistant, although not easy to recycle. It has many practical and aesthetic benefits, thus converting it into star material for hundreds of thousands of consumers who have ceased to be content with traditional materials frequently associated with outdated decorative aesthetics and styles. Its use in contemporary architecture has enabled its range of possible shapes, colors, and finishes to be increased dramatically. Plastic materials moreover have made practically any architectural solution affordable to all, which until recently was only available for those with the most generous of budgets. However, it is possible that the increase in the price of oil will have repercussions on that of plastic and its demand will diminish slightly over the next few years, giving way to new materials which contain the same properties, such as graphite, carbon fiber, or bio-plastic. *Plastic Design* contains dozens of examples and architectural projects which have used plastic in one or various of their features: walls, illumination, roofs, facades, furniture... The examples featured cover practically all the possible applications of plastic materials in contemporary architecture. In some of these examples the use of plastic can be seen straight away, whereas in others it adopts a more discreet and neutral appearance, which is a far throw from the aesthetic one we traditionally associate with this material (uniform textures, shiny or reflective finishes, bright colors). The result is as heterogeneous as the range of available plastics in the market is wide.

Während der letzten fünfzig Jahre hat die Kunststoffindustrie sich mit einem rasenden Tempo entwickelt, und sie ist in fast alle Lebensbereiche des Menschen eingedrungen, so auch in die Architektur. Dabei wurden Materialien wie Stahl und Eisen längst überholt. Das Wort Plastik leitet sich von dem griechischen Wort „plastikos" ab, das die Bedeutung „einfach zu formen" hat. Es handelt sich um ein organisches Polymer, manchmal um natürliche Stoffe wie Kautschuk oder Wachs, meist jedoch um synthetische oder halbsynthetische Stoffe, die aus langen makromolekularen Ketten bestehen, die in ihrer Struktur Kohlenstoff enthalten. Außerdem ist es ein billiges, flexibles, formbares, wasserundurchlässiges, isolierendes und widerstandsfähiges Material, das jedoch nur schwer recycelt werden kann. Es hat praktische und ästhetische Vorteile, weshalb es für Tausende von Verbrauchern zu einem der beliebtesten Materialien wurde. Für viele Produkte werden heutzutage keine traditionellen Materialien mehr verwendet, und diese traditionellen Materialien werden sogar oft mit einer Ästhetik und einem Dekorationsstil assoziiert, der aus der Mode gekommen ist. Die Verwendung von Kunststoff in der zeitgenössischen Architektur hat es möglich gemacht, dass viel mehr Formen, Farben und Oberflächen geschaffen werden können. Außerdem bieten Kunststoffe preisgünstige architektonische Lösungen auch für den bescheideneren Geldbeutel und es werden Ideen umgesetzt, die früher nur von denen verwirklicht wurden, die sich das leisten konnten. Dennoch wirkt sich die Erhöhung des Ölpreises auch auf den Kunststoffpreis aus, und die Verwendung ging in den letzten Jahren allmählich zurück. Neue Materialien mit den gleichen Eigenschaften werden eingesetzt, so zum Beispiel Graphit, Kohlenstofffasern oder Bioplastik. In *Plastic Design* finden Sie zahlreiche Beispiele und Bauprojekte, bei denen Kunststoff für ein oder mehrere Elemente verwendet wurde: Wände, Beleuchtung, Decken, Fassaden Möbel... Die ausgewählten Beispiele umfassen praktisch alle möglichen Anwendungen von Kunststoffen in der zeitgenössischen Architektur. Bei einigen dieser Beispiele erkennt man den Kunststoff auf den ersten Blick, während er in anderen Fällen ein neutrales und viel diskreteres Aussehen annimmt, das nichts mehr mit der Ästhetik zu tun hat, die man diesem Material ursprünglich zuschreibt, nämlich einheitliche Texturen, glänzende oder reflektierende Oberflächen und auffallende Farben. Das Ergebnis ist so vielseitig wie das Angebot an Kunststoffmaterialien auf dem Markt umfassend ist.

Durante los últimos cincuenta años la industria del plástico ha crecido a un ritmo brutal hasta alcanzar prácticamente todas las áreas de la actividad humana –incluida, evidentemente, la arquitectura–, superando fácilmente a la industria del acero y del hierro. El plástico, palabra derivada del griego *plastikos* (que quiere decir «fácil de moldear»), es un material orgánico polimérico, raramente natural (caucho o cera) y frecuentemente sintético o semisintético, formado por largas cadenas macromoleculares que contienen carbono en su estructura. Es además barato, flexible, moldeable, impermeable, aislante y resistente, aunque difícilmente reciclable; aúna ventajas prácticas y estéticas, por lo que se ha convertido en el material estrella para cientos de miles de consumidores que han dejado de conformarse con los materiales tradicionales, asociados frecuentemente a estéticas y estilos decorativos pasados de moda. Su uso en la arquitectura contemporánea ha permitido ampliar espectacularmente la gama de formas, colores y acabados posibles. Los materiales plásticos, además, han puesto al alcance de prácticamente cualquier economía soluciones arquitectónicas que hasta hace relativamente poco quedaban reservadas para los presupuestos más generosos. Sin embargo, es previsible que el aumento del precio del petróleo repercuta en el del plástico y su uso se resienta levemente durante los próximos años, cediendo algo de protagonismo a nuevos materiales que ostenten sus mismas propiedades (el grafito, la fibra de carbono o el bioplástico, por ejemplo). *Plastic Design* contiene decenas de ejemplos y de proyectos arquitectónicos que han recurrido al plástico en uno o varios de sus elementos: paredes, iluminación, cubiertas, fachadas, mobiliario... Los ejemplos escogidos cubren prácticamente todas las aplicaciones posibles de los materiales plásticos en la arquitectura contemporánea. En algunos de estos ejemplos el plástico puede localizarse a simple vista, mientras que en otros casos adopta una apariencia neutra, mucho más discreta, alejándose de la estética que tradicionalmente asociamos a este material (texturas uniformes, acabados brillantes o reflectantes, colorido llamativo). El resultado es tan heterogéneo como amplia es la gama de materiales plásticos disponible en el mercado.

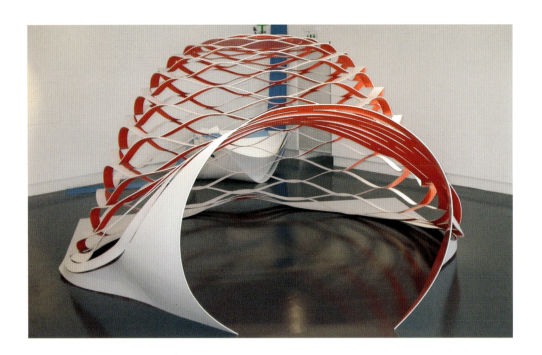

Au cours des 50 dernières années, l'industrie du plastique a connu une croissance brutale pour atteindre pratiquement tous les domaines de l'activité humaine, incluant bien entendu l'architecture, et dépassant facilement les industries de l'acier et du fer. Le plastique, mot dérivé du grec plastikos (qui signifie « facile à modeler »), est un matériau organique polymère, rarement naturel (caoutchouc ou cire) et fréquemment synthétique ou semi synthétique, formé de grandes chaînes macromoléculaires dont la structure contient du carbone. Il est également économique, flexible, modelable, imperméable, isolant et résistant, bien que difficilement recyclable. Il allie des vertus pratiques et esthétiques ce qui l'a converti en matériau étoile de centaines de milliers de consommateurs pour lesquels ne suffisent plus les matériaux traditionnels fréquemment associés, d'ailleurs, à des esthétiques et styles décoratifs passés de mode. Son usage dans l'architecture contemporaine a permis d'élargir la palette de formes, couleurs et finitions possibles. Les matériaux plastiques, en outre, ont mis à la portée de pratiquement toute économie des solutions architecturales qui, encore récemment, demeuraient réservées à des budgets plus généreux. Pour autant, il est prévisible que la hausse des cours du pétrole se répercute sur le prix du plastique et que son usage s'en ressente légèrement au cours des prochaines années, cédant la précédence à de nouveaux matériaux offrant les mêmes propriétés (graphite, fibre de carbone ou bioplastique par exemple). *Plastic Design* contient des dizaines d'exemples et de projets architecturaux ayant recouru au plastique dans un ou plusieurs de leurs éléments : murs, illumination, couvertes, façades, mobilier... Les exemples retenus couvrent pratiquement toutes les applications possibles des matières plastiques dans l'architecture contemporaine. Dans certains cas, le plastique est identifiable à première vue alors que, pour d'autres, il adopte une apparence neutre, bien plus discrète, s'éloignant de l'esthétique que nous associons traditionnellement à ce matériau (textures uniformes, finitions brillantes ou réfléchissantes, couleurs vivantes). Le résultat est aussi hétérogène que la gamme des matières plastiques disponibles sur le marché est ample.

Nel corso degli ultimi cinquant'anni l'industria della plastica è cresciuta ad un ritmo vertiginoso sino a raggiungere, in pratica, tutte le aree d'attività umana, ivi inclusa, evidentemente, l'architettura, e superando facilmente l'industria dell'acciaio e del ferro. La plastica, parola che deriva dal greco *plastikos* (che significa «facile da modellare»), è una materia organica polimerica, raramente naturale (caucciù o cera), e frequentemente sintetica o semisintetica, formata da lunghe catene macromolecolari che contengono nella loro struttura del carbonio. E' inoltre economica flessibile, modellabile, impermeabile, isolante e resistente, seppur difficilmente riciclabile, capace d'abbinare vantaggi pratici ed estetici, diventando per questo il materiale prescelto da centinaia di migliaia di consumatori che non si accontentano più dei materiali tradizionali, associati frequentemente ad estetiche e stili decorative passati di moda. Il suo uso nell'architettura contemporanea ha consentito d'ampliare in modo spettacolare la gamma delle forme, dei colori e delle possibili rifiniture. I materiali plastici, inoltre, hanno messo alla portata di qualsiasi economia, soluzioni architettoniche che, sino a relativamente poco tempo fa, erano riservate a budget più generosi. E' prevedibile, però, che l'aumento del costo del greggio abbia una ripercussione su quello della plastica e che nel corso dei prossimi anni il suo uso possa lievemente risentirne cedendo un po' di protagonismo a nuovi materiali che ostentano le sue stesse proprietà (la grafite, la fibra di carbonio o la bioplastica, per esempio). *Plastic Design* contiene decine d'esempi e di progetti architettonici che hanno fatto ricorso alla plastica in uno o vari dei loro elementi: pareti, illuminazione, coperture, facciate, mobili... Gli esempi prescelti coprono, in pratica, tutte le applicazioni possibili dei materiali plastici nell'architettura contemporanea. In alcuni di questi esempi, la plastica salta subito alla vista, mentre in altri casi la sua presenza rimane neutra, molto più discreta, lungi dall'estetica tradizionalmente associata a questo materiale (consistenze uniformi, finiture brillanti e riflettenti, colori squillanti). Il risultato è tanto eterogeneo quanto amplia è la gamma dei materiali plastici disponibili sul mercato.

This loft, an old warehouse in the port of Rotterdam, was conceived as an open two level space. The padded colored panels, made from polyether and skai have a triple function: they serve firstly as door to the kids bedroom, secondly as the front part of a hidden library and thirdly as sound proofing. The bath has been covered with 30 mm thick epoxy resin panels.

Dieses Loft, ein ehemaliges Lager im Hafen von Rotterdam, wurde als ein offener Raum auf zwei Ebenen angelegt. Die gepolsterten, farbigen Paneele aus Polyether und Kunstleder erfüllen eine dreifache Funktion. Sie dienen als Tür für das Kinderzimmer, als Vorderseite für die versteckte Bibliothek und zur akustischen Isolierung. Die Badewanne wurde mit 30 Millimeter dicken Paneelen aus Expoxydharz verkleidet.

Este loft, un antiguo almacén del puerto de Rotterdam, ha sido concebido como un espacio abierto de dos niveles. Los coloridos paneles acolchados, fabricados con poliéter y escay, tienen una triple función: actúan como puerta para el dormitorio infantil, como frontal para una librería oculta y como aislantes acústicos. La bañera ha sido recubierta con paneles de resina epoxídica de 30 milímetros de grosor.

Ce loft, un ancien magasin du port de Rotterdam, a été conçu comme un espace ouvert de deux niveaux. Les panneaux colorés rembourrés, fabriqués en polyester et en skaï, remplissent une triple fonction : ils servent de porte pour la chambre d'enfant, de frontal d'une bibliothèque escamotée et d'isolation phonique. La baignoire a été recouverte de panneaux de résine époxy de 30 millimètres d'épaisseur.

Questo loft, un vecchio magazzino del porto di Rotterdam, è stato concepito come spazio aperto a due livelli. I pannelli colorati imbottiti, prodotti in poliestere e sky, hanno una triplice funzione: servono da porta per la stanza del bambino, da frontale di una libreria nascosta e da isolante acustico. La vasca da bagno è stata ricoperta con pannelli di resina epossidica di 30 millimetri di spessore.

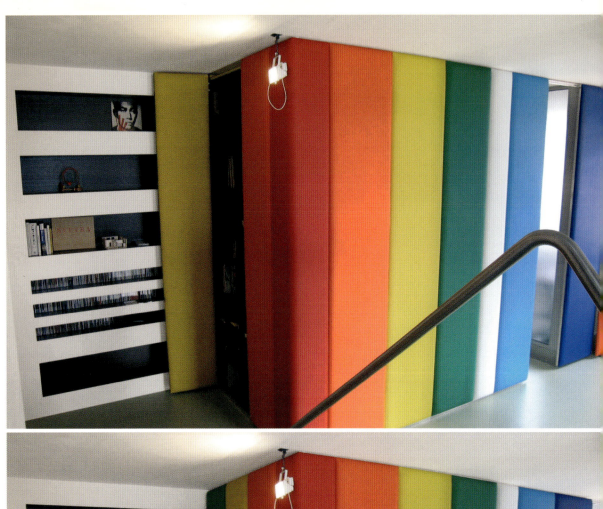

The curved walls of this business school which give it an organic appearance, as well as giving movement to the interior spaces, have been made from a plastic mesh, decorated with photographs of floral motifs. The colors of these photographs help to visually distinguish the different areas of the school.

Die gebogenen Wände dieser Handelsschule lassen das Gebäude organisch wirken und die Innenräume scheinen sich in Bewegung zu befinden. Diese Wände wurden aus einem Kunststoffnetz konstruiert, das an einigen Stellen von Fotografien mit Blumenmotiven bedeckt ist. Die Farben dieser Fotos unterscheiden visuell die verschiedenen Räume der Schule.

Las paredes curvas de esta escuela de negocios, que le confieren una apariencia orgánica y dotan de movimiento a los espacios interiores, han sido fabricadas con una malla plástica, recubierta en algunos puntos con fotografías de motivos florales. Los colores de esas fotografías ayudan a distinguir visualmente los diferentes espacios de la escuela.

Les parois courbes de cette école de commerce, qui lui confèrent une apparence organique tout en dotant de mouvement les espaces intérieurs, ont été fabriquées avec une maille plastique recouverte par endroits de photographies de motifs floraux. Les couleurs de ces imprimés aident à distinguer visuellement les différents espaces de l'école.

Le pareti curve di questa Business School che gli conferiscono un'apparenza organica, dotando di movimento gli spazi interni, sono state fabbricate con una maglia plastica, ricoperta in alcuni punti con foto di motivi floreali. I colori delle fotografie aiutano a distinguere visivamente i vari spazi della scuola.

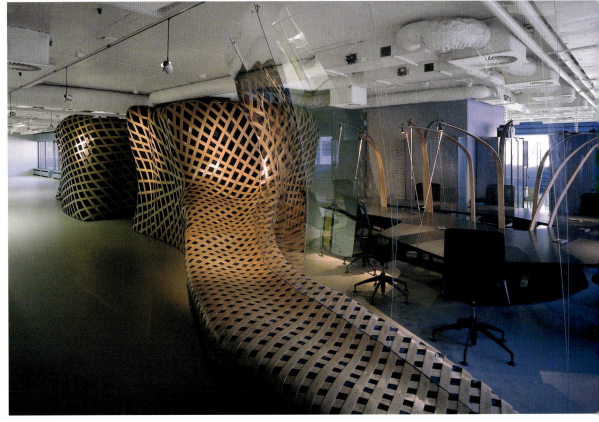

ALDEN MADDRY | NEW YORK
PHILLIPPS SKAIFE RESIDENCE
New York, USA | 2001

The bathroom of this New York apartment has been separated from the living room by a Plexiglas and aluminum wall which serves as a box of light. The Plexiglas is translucent in some parts and this brings the color fittings of the bathroom into view. The wall is made of two layers of Plexiglas fitted onto the aluminum structure – the one facing the bathroom is orange and the one facing the lounge is white.

Das Badezimmer dieses Appartements in New York wurde vom Wohnzimmer durch eine Plexiglaswand und Aluminium getrennt, so dass eine Art Lichtkasten entstand. An einigen Stellen der Wand ist das Plexiglas lichtdurchlässig, so dass man die Farbe der Badezimmerwände erkennen kann. Die Wand besteht aus zwei Schichten Plexiglas, die auf eine Aluminiumstruktur montiert sind. Die Seite zum Badezimmer hin ist orange, und die zum Wohnzimmer weiß.

El cuarto de baño de este apartamento neoyorquino ha sido separado de la sala de estar por medio de una pared de plexiglás y aluminio que actúa como una caja de luz. En algunas partes de esa pared el plexiglás es translúcido, lo cual permite apreciar el color de los revestimientos del cuarto de baño. La pared se compone de dos capas de plexiglás montadas sobre una estructura de aluminio: la que da al cuarto de baño es naranja; la que da a la sala de estar, blanca.

La salle de bains de cet appartement new-yorkais a été séparée du séjour au moyen d'une paroi de plexiglas et d'aluminium jouant les caisses de lumière. En certains endroits de cette paroi, le plexiglas se fait translucide, permettant ainsi d'apprécier la couleur des revêtements de la salle de bains. La paroi se compose de deux couches de plexiglas montées sur la structure d'aluminium : celle donnant sur la salle de bains est orange, celle du séjour est blanche.

Il bagno di quest'appartamento di New York, è stato separato dal salone da una parete in plexiglas ed alluminio che funge da scatola di luce. In alcuni punti di questa parete, il plexiglas è translucido, cosa che consente d'apprezzare il colore dei rivestimenti del bagno. La parete è composta di due strati di plexiglas montati su una struttura d'alluminio: quella che da sul bagno è arancione e quella sul salone, bianca.

The interior fittings of this rehabilitation center for drug addicts in Utrecht, are a high pressure laminate (HPL) and have been covered with large size photographs of ivy to soften the transition between the exterior and interior of the building and to make it more comfortable for the patients.

Die Innenverkleidungen in diesem Rehabilitationszentrum für Drogenabhängige in Utrecht bestehen aus einem Hochdrucklaminat (HPL) und sind mit großformatigen Efeu-Fotografien bedeckt. So scheint der Übergang von außen nach innen weniger abrupt zu sein und die Umgebung wirkt auf die Insassen harmonisch.

Los revestimientos interiores de este centro de rehabilitación para drogadictos de Utrecht, fabricados con un laminado de alta presión (HPL), han sido recubiertos con grandes fotografías de hiedras, para suavizar el tránsito entre el exterior y el interior del edificio y hacerlo así más llevadero para los internos.

Les revêtements intérieurs de ce centre de réhabilitation pour toxicomanes d'Utrecht, en réalité un laminé haute pression (HPL), ont été recouverts de grandes photographies de lierre pour adoucir la transition entre l'extérieur et l'intérieur de l'édifice et le rendre ainsi plus supportable pour les internes.

I rivestimenti interni di questo centro di recupero per tossicodipendenti d'Utrecht, fabbricati con un laminato ad alta pressione (HPL), sono stati ricoperti di foto d'edera in gran formato, per ammorbidire il passaggio tra l'esterno e l'interno dell'edificio, rendendolo così più gradevole.

The Mobilebox, an ironic solution in the creation of a traditional house in a constantly changing world, was conceived as a mobile meeting and information space for the town council of the new Dutch town Leidsche Rijn. The exterior walls of the Mobilebox are polyester panels which imitate the traditional shape of mud bricks.

Die Mobilebox ist eine ironische Antwort auf die Notwendigkeit, in der heutigen Welt des ständigen Wandels über ein traditionelles Haus verfügen zu müssen. Sie wurde als eine mobiler Versammlungsort und Informationspunkt für die Stadtverwaltung der „neuen" holländischen Stadt Leidsche Rijn entworfen. Die Außenwände der Mobilebox werden von Polyesterpaneelen gebildet, die die Formen der traditionellen Ziegelsteine imitieren.

La Mobilebox, una respuesta irónica a la necesidad de contar con una casa tradicial en un mundo en constante transformación, ha sido concebida como espacio móvil de reunión e información para el ayuntamiento de la «nueva» ciudad holandesa de Leidsche Rijn. Las paredes exteriores de la Mobilebox son paneles de poliéster que imitan la forma de los tradicionales ladrillos de barro.

La Mobilebox, une réponse ironique à la nécessité de disposer d'une maison additionnelle dans un monde en évolution permanente, a été conçue comme un espace mobile de réunion et d'information pour la municipalité de la « ville nouvelle » hollandaise de Leidsche Rijn. Les parois extérieures de la Mobilebox sont des panneaux de polyester imitant la forme des briques traditionnelles.

La Mobilebox, risposta ironica alla necessità di una casa tradizionale in un mondo in costante trasformazione, è stata concepita come spazio mobile di riunione ed informazione per il comune della «nuova» cittadina olandese di Leidsche Rijn. Le pareti esterne della Mobilebox sono dei pannelli in poliestere che imitano la forma dei tradizionali mattoni di cotto.

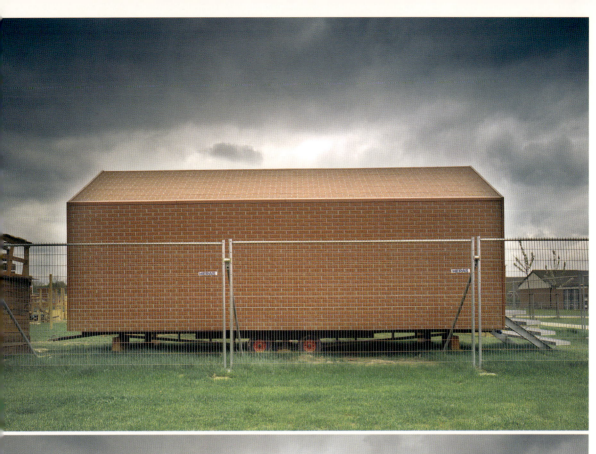

The central element of the Genzyme Center, an office building housing 920 people, shops, a restaurant and public access areas, is an impressive illumination system reminiscent of the traditional spider lamps and is made from hundreds of small plastic sheets.

Das zentrale Element des Genzyme Centers, ein Bürogebäude für 920 Personen mit Geschäften, einem Restaurant und öffentliche zugänglichen Räumen, ist das beeindruckende Verstärkungssystem für die Beleuchtung, das an traditionelle Kronleuchter erinnert und aus hunderten von kleinen Plastikstreifen besteht.

El elemento central del Genzyme Center —un edificio de oficinas para 920 personas que incluye tiendas, un restaurante y espacios de acceso público— es un impresionante sistema de refuerzo de la iluminación que recuerda las tradicionales lámparas de araña y que está formado por centenares de pequeñas láminas de plástico.

L'élément central du Genzyme Center, un immeuble de bureaux pour 920 personnes comprenant des boutiques, un restaurant et des espaces publics, est un système impressionnant de renfort de l'illumination qui rappelle les lustres traditionnels et formé de centaines de petites feuilles de plastique.

L'elemento centrale del Genzyme Center —un edificio d'uffici per 920 persone con negozi, un ristorante, e spazi d'accesso pubblico— è un impressionante sistema di rinforzo dell'illuminazione che ricorda i tradizionali lampadari a ragno, composto da centinaia di piccole lamine di plastica.

BOHLIN CYWINSKI JACKSON | SEATTLE
GOSLINE HOUSE
Seattle, USA | 2000

The polycarbonate screens – made using a very resistant thermoplastic polymer – enhance the natural light and the views of the surrounding scenery. The polycarbonate panels extend to the interior of the dwelling where they function in the same way as those in the exterior.

Die Schirme aus Polykarbonat, ein thermoplastisches Polymer, das sehr schlagfest ist, wurden in diesem Gebäude benutzt, damit viel Licht einfallen und man die umgebende Landschaft betrachten kann. Die Polykarbonatpaneele erstrecken sich bis in das Innere des Hauses, wo sie die gleichen Funktionen erfüllen wie außen.

Las pantallas de policarbonato, un polímero termoplástico con una excelente resistencia a los impactos, han sido utilizadas en esta residencia con el objeto de permitir la entrada en ella de la mayor cantidad de luz posible, así como de facilitar la observación del paisaje circundante. Los paneles de policarbonato se extienden hasta el interior de la vivienda, donde cumplen las mismas funciones que en el exterior.

Les écrans de polycarbonate, un polymère thermoplastique présentant une excellente résistance à l'impact, ont été utilisés dans cette résidence dans l'objectif d'y permettre l'entrée de la quantité la plus grande possible de lumière, tout en facilitant l'observation du paysage environnant. Les panneaux de polycarbonate s'étendent jusqu'à l'intérieur de la demeure où ils remplissent les mêmes fonctions qu'à l'extérieur.

Gli schermi in policarbonato, un polimero termoplastico con un'eccellente resistenza agli impatti, sono stati usati in questa casa per consentire il massimo afflusso di luce, e permettere d'osservare il paesaggio circostante. I pannelli di policarbonato si estendono sino all'interno della casa, ove hanno le stesse funzioni dell'esterno.

In the attractive loft of the Brazilian singer Maisa Matarazzo plastic is used as a common denominator throughout the dwelling. This gives the loft visual unity and bestows on it a unique ambience, combining the 60's pop aesthetic and the most avant-garde tendencies of contemporary interior design.

In dem auffallenden Loft der brasilianischen Sängerin Maísa Matarazzo hat man Kunststoff als wiederholendes Element in allen Räumen benutzt, um eine visuelle Einheitlichkeit zu schaffen. So entstand eine ganz besondere Atmosphäre in einem Stil zwischen der Pop-Art der Sechzigerjahre und den avantgardistischsten Trends moderner Innenarchitektur.

En el llamativo loft de la cantante brasileña Maísa Matarazzo se ha recurrido al plástico como elemento común de todos sus espacios, lo que le confiere unidad visual y le dota de una peculiar atmósfera a medio camino de la estética pop de los años sesenta y de las tendencias más vanguardistas del diseño de interiores contemporáneo.

Le loft saisissant de la chanteuse brésilienne Maísa Matarazzo a vu l'emploi du plastique comme élément commun de tous ses espaces, ce qui lui confère une identité visuelle et le dote d'une atmosphère particulière à mi-chemin de l'esthétique pop des années 60 et des tendances les plus avant-gardistes du design d'intérieur contemporain.

Nell'originale loft della cantante brasiliana Maísa Matarazzo, si è ricorsi alla plastica come elemento comune di tutti gli spazi, cosa che gli conferisce un'unità visiva, dotandolo di una particolare atmosfera a metà strada tra l'estetica pop degli anni sessanta e le tendenze più avanguardiste del design d'interni contemporaneo.

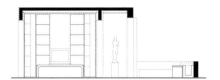

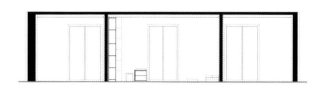

BURATTI-BATTISTON ARCHITECTS | MILAN
A.SHOP, Intermot Fair
Munich, Germany | 2004

Acerbis Italia is a company specializing in the manufacture and commercialization of sport products for motorcycling events. The Buratti-Battison architect firm created a flexible system of plastic modules specifically for them to use in trade fairs and shops. The unique anchorage system enables the creation of walls, shelves, storage space and other similar structures.

Acerbis Italia ist ein auf die Herstellung und den Vertrieb von Artikeln für den Motorsport spezialisiertes Unternehmen. Das Atelierstudio Buratti-Battiston hat für dieses Unternehmen ein flexibles, modulares Kunststoffsystem entwickelt, das für Messen und Shops bestimmt ist. Mit Hilfe des speziellen Verankerungssystems kann man sowohl Wände als auch Regale, Lagerräume oder ähnliche Strukturen schaffen.

Acerbis Italia es una empresa especializada en la fabricación y comercialización de productos deportivos para el mundo del motociclismo. El despacho de arquitectos Buratti-Battiston ha creado especialmente para ellos un flexible sistema modular de plástico pensado para ferias y tiendas, cuyo peculiar sistema de anclaje permite construir tanto paredes como estanterías, espacios de almacenaje o cualquier otra estructura similar.

Acerbis Italia est une entreprise spécialisée dans la fabrication et la commercialisation de produits sportifs pour le monde de la moto. Le cabinet d'architectes Buratti-Battiston a créé spécialement pour eux un système modulaire flexible de plastique pensé pour les foires et expositions. Son dispositif d'ancrage particulier permet de construire aussi bien des parois que des étagères, des espaces de rangement ou toute autre structure similaire.

Acerbis Italia è una ditta specializzata nella fabbricazione e vendita di prodotti sportivi per il mondo del motociclismo. Lo studio degli architetti Buratti-Battiston ha creato per loro un sistema modulare di plastica flessibile ideato per fiere e negozi, con un peculiare sistema d'ancoraggio che permette di costruire pareti come scaffalature, spazi di stoccaggio o qualsiasi altra struttura simile.

CONCRETE ARCHITECTURAL ASSOCIATES | AMSTERDAM
THE MANSION
Amsterdam, The Netherlands | 2004

Conceived from a vague briefing which included only the adjectives «luxurious, classic, sexy, chic and warm», the men's club «The Mansion» boasts walls covered with vinyl. The color of the vinyl varies depending on the room, favoring different moods and creating diverse ambiences in each of the 12 spaces which makes up the club.

Nach einem sehr knappen „Briefing", bei dem nur die Adjektive „luxuriös, klassisch, sexy, schick und warm" genannt wurden, gibt es in dem Herrenclub The Mansion unter anderem auch Wände, die mit Vinyl verkleidet sind. Die Farbe dieses Materials ändert sich in jedem Raum. So werden in jedem der zwölf Räume des Klubs verschiedene Eindrücke geschaffen und andere Gefühle hervorgerufen.

Concebido a partir de un escueto *briefing* que sólo incluía los adjetivos «lujoso, clásico, sexy, chic y cálido», el club de caballeros The Mansion cuenta, entre otros elementos, con paredes empapeladas con vinilo. El color de este vinilo varía en función de la estancia, favoreciendo distintos estados de ánimo y creando atmósferas dispares en cada uno de los doce espacios que componen el club.

Conçu à partir d'un briefing succinct qui incluait uniquement les adjectifs « luxueux, classique, sexy, chic et chaleureux », le club pour hommes The Mansion compte, notamment, des parois revêtues de vinyle. La couleur de ce vinyle varie selon la pièce, favorisant divers états d'esprit et créant des atmosphères différenciées dans chacun des 12 espaces composant le lieu.

Concepito con un semplice *briefing* che includeva solo gli aggettivi «lussuoso, classico, sexy, chic e caldo», il club per uomini The Mansion presenta, tra i tanti elementi, delle pareti rivestite di vinile. Il colore di questo vinile varia in funzione della stanza, favorendo vari stati d'animo e creando diverse atmosfere in ognuno dei dodici spazi del club.

CREPAIN BINST ARCHITECTURE/JO CREPAIN | ANTWERP
DUVAL GUILLAUME
Brussels, Belgium | 2001

Duval Guillaume is an advertising agency with a great deal of experience in radio and television. From the reception area and the lower floor of its Brussels HQ the main attraction of the building is in full view – an impressive 16 m high atrium complete with a glass dome. The eye-catching panels of wavy Plexiglas are situated on its base and have neon lights behind them which illuminate the space and give it a rather futuristic feel.

Duval Guillaume ist eine Werbeagentur mit viel Erfahrung im Bereich Radio und Fernsehwerbung. Von der Rezeption und dem Erdgeschoss ihres Sitzes in Brüssel aus kann man sehr gut das schönste Element des Gebäudes sehen, ein beeindruckender, fast 16 Meter hoher Hof, der von einer Glaskuppel bedeckt ist. Unten in diesem Hof befinden sich zwei auffallende Paneele aus gewellten Plexiglas. Dahinter beleuchten mehrere Neonlichter den Raum und lassen ihn so fast futuristisch wirken.

Duval Guillaume es una agencia de publicidad con gran experiencia en radio y televisión. Desde la recepción o planta inferior de su sede de Bruselas puede observarse perfectamente el principal atractivo del edificio: un espectacular atrio de casi 16 metros de alto, coronado por una cúpula de cristal. En su base se encuentran dos llamativos paneles de plexiglás ondulado. Tras ellos, varias luces de neón iluminan el espacio dotándolo de una atmósfera casi futurista.

Duval Guillaume est une agence de publicité très expérimentée en radio et tv. Depuis la réception ou le niveau inférieur de son siège de Bruxelles, il est loisible d'observer parfaitement l'attrait principal de l'édifice : un spectaculaire atrium de près de 16 mètres de haut couronné d'une coupole vitrée. Sa base accueille deux saisissants panneaux de plexiglas ondulé. Derrière, plusieurs lumières au néon illuminent l'espace en le dotant d'une atmosphère presque futuriste.

Duval Guillaume è un'agenzia di pubblicità con grand'esperienza in radio e televisione. Dalla reception o il piano inferiore della sua sede di Bruxelles, si può osservare perfettamente l'elemento di maggior interesse dell'edificio: uno spettacolare atrio di quasi 16 metri d'altezza rifinito da una cupola di vetro. Alla base, vi sono due vistosi pannelli di plexiglas ondulato. Dietro, varie luci al neon illuminano lo spazio conferendogli un'atmosfera quasi futurista.

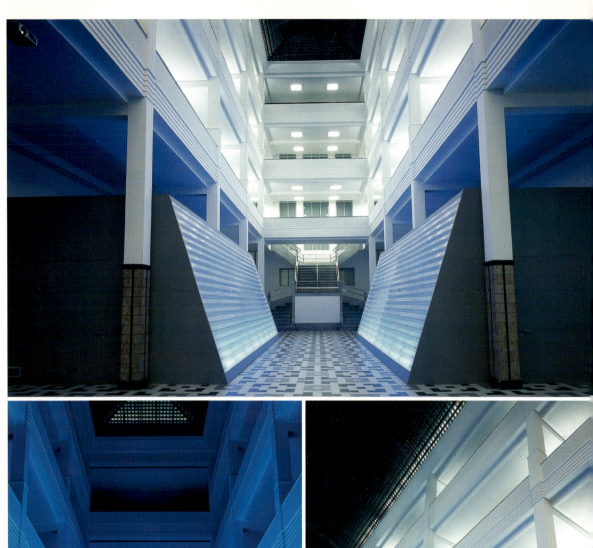

CREPAIN BINST ARCHITECTURE/JO CREPAIN | ANTWERP
FEYEN RESIDENCE
Sint-Piers-Leeuw, Belgium | 2000

The 7 x 12,50 m lounge with a total height of 3,30 m for a family of four houses a cube shaped central structure in which is housed the kitchen and work area. The walls of the structure are actually opalescent polycarbonate laminas which are illuminated by fluorescent lights. At night the structure, seen from a distance, resembles a huge ice cube.

Das 7 x 12,50 Meter große und 3,30 Meter hohe Wohnzimmer im Wohnhaus einer vierköpfigen Familie beherbergt einen zentralen, würfelförmigen Körper, in dem sich die Küche und das Arbeitszimmer befinden. Die Wände dieses Körpers sind in Wirklichkeit Leisten aus opalisierendem Plexiglas, die mit Leuchtstoffröhren beleuchtet werden. Nachts wirkt dieser Körper von außen gesehen wie ein riesiger Eiswürfel.

El salón –de 7 x 12,50 metros y de 3,30 metros de altura– de esta vivienda para una familia de cuatro miembros alberga un volumen central en forma de cubo en el que se ha integrado la cocina y el espacio de trabajo. Las paredes del volumen son en realidad láminas de policarbonato opalescente iluminado por luces fluorescentes. Por la noche, el volumen parece, visto desde el exterior de la vivienda, un cubo de hielo gigante.

Le salon de 7 x 12,50 mètres et 3,30 mètres de haut de cette demeure d'une famille de quatre membres héberge un volume central en forme de cube où ont été intégrés la cuisine et l'espace de travail. Les parois du volume sont en réalité des feuilles de polycarbonate opalescent, illuminé par des lumières fluorescentes. De nuit, le volume ressemble, vu de l'extérieur de la maison, à un cube de glace géant.

Il salone –di 7 x 12,50 metri e 3,30 metri d'altezza– di questa casa per una famiglia di 4 membri dispone di un volume centrale a forma di cubo che integra la cucina e lo spazio da lavoro. Le pareti del volume sono in realtà lamine di policarbonato opalescente illuminate da luci fluorescenti. Di notte, il volume pare, visto dall'esterno della casa, un cubo di ghiaccio gigante.

In the cake shop C-3 the attractively colored walls and the plastic cakes sum up the essence of the shop and catch the client's attention which is then, once inside, diverted to the real, edible cakes inside the transparent counter. The result is a contemporary space with an avant-garde take on the traditional cake shop.

In der Konditorei C-3 fassen die starken Farben der Wände und die Torten aus Kunststoff die Essenz des Lokals zusammen und ziehen die Aufmerksamkeit der Kunden auf sich. Sobald man sich in der Konditorei befindet, schaut man auf die Torten, und zwar auf die echten und essbaren Torten in der transparenten Theke. So entstand eine zeitgemäße, fast avantgardistische Umgebung als Neuinterpretation traditioneller Konditoreien.

En la pastelería C-3 los llamativos colores de las paredes y los pasteles de plástico resumen la esencia del local y atraen la atención del cliente, que rápidamente, y una vez ya en el interior, dirige la vista hacia los pasteles (esta vez reales y comestibles) del mostrador transparente. El resultado es un espacio contemporáneo y casi vanguardista en su reinterpretación de las tradicionales pastelerías.

Dans la pâtisserie C-3, les couleurs vives des murs et les gâteaux de plastique résument l'essence des lieux et attirent l'attention de la clientèle qui, une fois à l'intérieur, porte rapidement le regard sur les gâteaux (cette fois réels et comestibles) de la vitrine transparente. Il en résulte un espace contemporain et presque avant-gardiste dans sa réinterprétation des pâtisseries traditionnelles.

Nella pasticceria C-3 i colori sgargianti delle pareti ed i dolci di plastica riassumono l'essenza del locale e colpiscono l'attenzione del cliente, che rapidamente, una volta dentro, rivolge lo sguardo verso i dolci (questa volta veri e commestibili) del bancone trasparente. Il risultato è uno spazio contemporaneo, quasi avanguardista nella sua re-interpretazione delle pasticcerie tradizionali.

The light sources in the bathroom of this loft have been concealed behind a metal structure covered with laminates of Plexiglas. This material meets all the necessary requisites for this project: it is a translucent material, damp resistant, elastic, visually attractive, modern and inexpensive. Moreover, in this case, it serves as a light box, giving the space a futuristic feel.

Die Lichtquellen im Badezimmer dieses Lofts wurden hinter einer Metallstruktur verborgen, die mit Plexiglasstreifen verkleidet ist. Plexiglas erfüllt alle notwendigen Voraussetzungen für die geplante Verwendung. Es handelt sich um ein lichtdurchlässiges, feuchtigkeitsbeständiges, elastisches, visuell anziehendes, modernes und preisgünstiges Material. In diesem Fall wurde eine Art Lichtkasten geschaffen, der den Raum futuristisch wirken lässt.

Las fuentes de luz del cuarto de baño de este loft han sido ocultadas tras una estructura metálica recubierta con láminas de plexiglás. El plexiglás cumplía todos los requisitos necesarios para este proyecto: es un material translúcido, resistente a la humedad, elástico, visualmente atractivo, moderno y barato. En este caso, además, actúa como una caja de luz, confiriéndole al espacio una atmósfera futurista.

Les fontaines de lumière de la salle de bains de ce loft ont été occultées derrière une structure métallique couverte de feuilles de plexiglas. Le plexiglas remplissait toutes les conditions nécessaires au projet : il s'agit d'un matériau translucide, résistant à l'humidité, élastique, séduisant visuellement, moderne et économique. En l'occurrence, il agit comme une caisse de lumière conférant à l'espace une atmosphère futuriste.

I punti luce del bagno di questo loft sono stati nascosti da una struttura metallica ricoperta da lamine di plexiglas. Il plexiglas offriva tutti i requisiti necessari per questo progetto: è un materiale translucido, resistente all'umidità, elastico, visivamente attraente, moderno, ed economico. In questo caso, inoltre, funge anche da cassa di luce, conferendo allo spazio un'atmosfera futurista.

DESAI-CHIA ARCHITECTURE/KATHERINE CHIA | NEW YORK
FLOWER DISTRICT LOFT
New York, USA | 2003

This loft, belonging to a young Hindu businessman, was conceived in such way so as to be able to house parties for around 100 people and also as a conventional family dwelling. The doors, leaded glass and plastic panels within an aluminum frame draw inspiration from the traditional Hindu jali and allow the free flow of light between the private and public areas of the loft.

Dieses Loft gehört einem jungen, indischen Unternehmer und wurde so geplant, dass Feste für ungefähr hundert Personen stattfinden können, es aber kurz darauf wieder zu einer traditionellen Wohnung für eine Familie wird. Die Türen, mit Paneelen aus mit Säure behandeltem Glas und Kunststoff in Aluminiumrahmen sind visuell von der indischen Jali-Technik inspiriert, und lassen Licht in alle privaten und gemeinsam genutzten Räume des Lofts.

Este loft, perteneciente a un joven empresario hindú, ha sido concebido de manera que pueda albergar fiestas para unas cien personas y convertirse poco después en una vivienda familiar convencional. Las puertas, los paneles de vidrio al ácido y los de plástico encajados en un marco de aluminio se inspiran visualmente en el tradicional jali hindú, y permiten el libre flujo de la luz entre las áreas privadas y las públicas del loft.

Ce loft, propriété d'un jeune entrepreneur indien, a été conçu de sorte à pouvoir accueillir des fêtes pour 100 personnes et se convertir ensuite rapidement en une demeure familiale conventionnelle. Les portes, panneaux de verre à l'acide et de plastique insérés dans un cadre d'aluminium, s'inspirent visuellement du traditionnel Jali indien et permettent le flux libre de la lumière entre les parties privées et publiques du loft.

Questo loft di un giovane imprenditore hindu è stato concepito in modo tale da poter accogliere feste per circa cento persone, e diventare, poco dopo, una casa familiare convenzionale. Le porte, i pannelli in vetro all'acido e quelli di plastica inseriti in infissi d'alluminio s'ispirano visivamente al tradizionale jali hindu, consentendo alla luce di passare liberamente tra le zone private e pubbliche del loft.

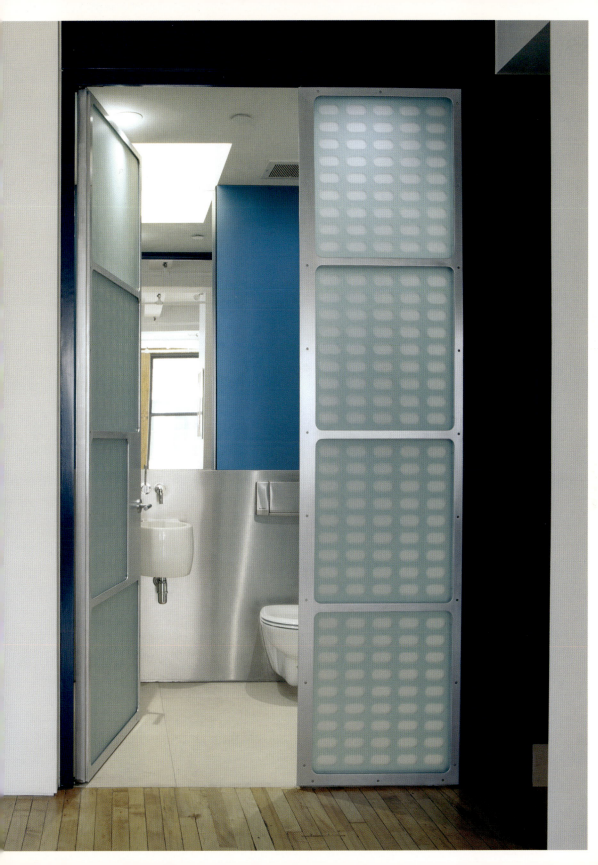

Plastic was chosen as the key material for various features in this Hanover café (the chairs and the counter) because of its numerous practical benefits, and as homage to the innovative plastic floors designed in 1939 by the architect Vilhelm Lauritzen for Copenhagen airport. The result is a fluid, modern and functional space despite its deep long shape.

Kunststoff wurde aufgrund der Vorteile, die es zu bieten hat, als Hauptmaterial für verschiedene Elemente in diesem Café in Hannover gewählt (Stühle, Theke). Gleichzeitig erinnert es an die innovativen Böden aus Kunststoff, die der Architekt Vilhelm Lauritzen 1939 für den Flughafen von Kopenhagen konstruieren ließ. So entstand ein moderner und funktioneller Raum, der trotz seiner länglichen und tiefen Form fließend wirkt.

El plástico ha sido escogido como el material principal de varios elementos de este café de Hanóver (sillas, mostrador) por sus innumerables ventajas prácticas; asimismo, esta elección es un homenaje a los innovadores suelos de material plástico diseñados en 1939 por el arquitecto Vilhelm Lauritzen para el aeropuerto de Copenhague. El resultado es un espacio moderno y funcional que fluye suavemente a pesar de su forma alargada y profunda.

Le plastique a été choisi comme matériau principal de divers éléments de ce café de Hanovre (chaises, comptoir) en raison de ses innombrables avantages pratiques, ainsi qu'en hommage aux sols novateurs en matière plastique créés en 1939 par l'architecte Vilhelm Lauritzen pour l'aéroport de Copenhague. Naît un espace moderne et fonctionnel, doucement fluide en dépit de sa forme allongée et profonde.

La plastica è stata scelta come materiale principale di vari elementi di questo caffè d'Hannover (sedie del bancone) per i suoi innumerevoli vantaggi pratici, ma anche come omaggio ai pavimenti in materiale plastico innovativi disegnati nel 1939 dall'architetto Vilhelm Lauritzen per l'aeroporto di Copenhaguen. Il risultato è uno spazio moderno e funzionale che scorre leggermente nonostante la sua forma allungata e profonda.

The blue polycarbonate panels separate the different spaces of the ImageNet offices and strengthen the concept of office and warehouse as one. The use of materials such as vinyl and cement transmits the idea of «inexpensively inventive». The network of cables hanging from the ceiling is a metaphor of the work carried out there – the conversion of chaos into useful information for the client.

Die Paneele aus blauem Polykarbonat unterteilen die verschiedenen Büroräume von ImageNet und unterstreichen so den Eindruck des Zusammenhangs zwischen Büro und Lager. Die Verwendung von Materialien wie Vinyl und Zement unterstreicht die Idee von „innovativ, aber preisgünstig". Das Kabelnetz, das an der Decke hängt, ist eine Metapher auf die Arbeit, der man sich in diesem Büro widmet, der Umformung des Chaos in nützliche Information für den Kunden.

Los paneles de policarbonato azul dividen los distintos espacios de las oficinas de ImageNet y refuerzan la idea de cohabitación entre oficina y almacén. El uso de materiales como el vinilo o el cemento transmite la idea de «inventiva a bajo coste» que se pretende comunicar. La red de cables que cuelga del techo es, por otro lado, una metáfora del trabajo realizado en la oficina: la conversión del caos en información útil para el cliente.

Les panneaux de polycarbonate bleus divisent les divers espaces des bureaux d'ImageNet et renforcent l'idée de cohabitation entre les bureaux et les magasins. L'usage de matériaux comme le vinyle ou le ciment transmet l'idée d'esprit « inventif à bas prix » qu'il prétend communiquer. Le réseau de câbles qui pend du plafond est, à son tour, une métaphore du travail réalisé dans les bureaux: la conversion du chaos en information utile pour le client.

I pannelli di policarbonato blu dividono i vari spazi degli uffici ImageNet e rafforzano l'idea della coabitazione tra uffici e magazzino. L'uso di materiali come il vinile od il cemento trasmettono l'idea d'«inventiva a basso costo» che si vuole comunicare. La rete di cavi appesi al soffitto è, d'altra parte, una metafora del lavoro che si svolge nell'ufficio: la conversione del caos in informazioni utili per il cliente.

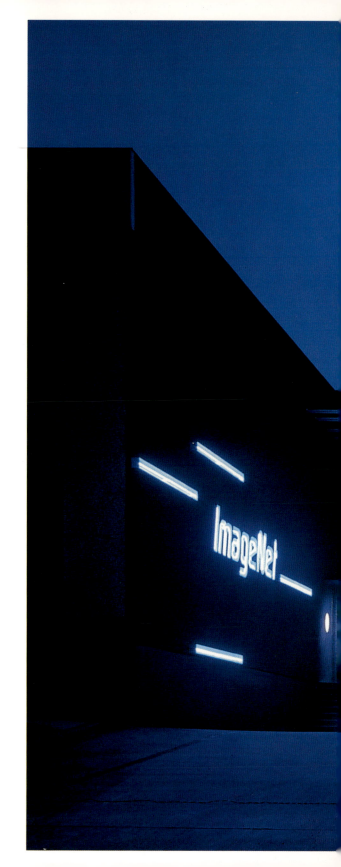

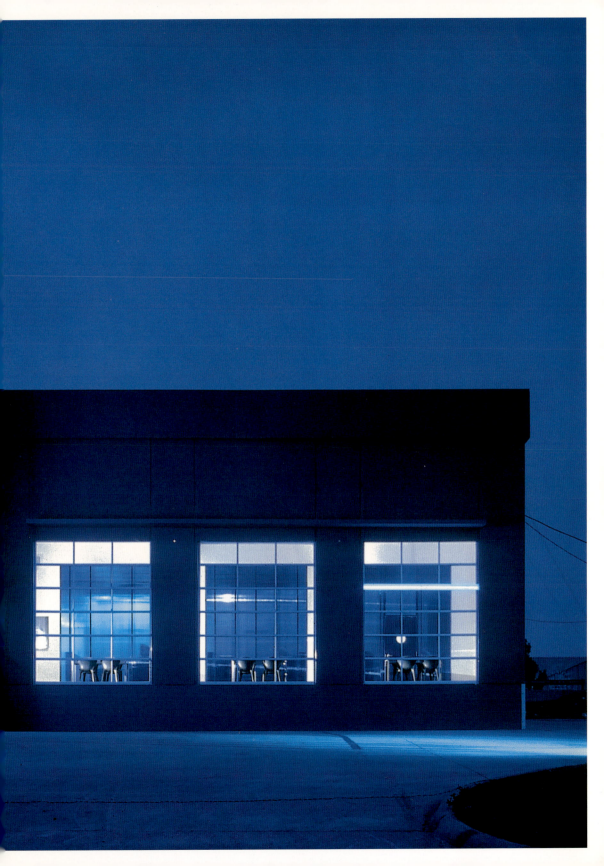

"The successful
companies of the
next decade will
be the ones that
use digital tools to
reinvent the way
they work. These
companies will
make decisions
quickly, act
efficiently, and
directly touch
their customers in
positive ways."

Bill Gates, 1999

The relocation of the ImageNet HQ in Oklahoma, from the lower level of a garage to its new setting and the use of plastic and acrylic materials has enabled the company to renovate its corporate image. It has been converted into a company which transmits efficiency, modernity, speed and professionalism. The change of HQ and the renovation of its corporate image has led to the signing of the biggest contract in the history of the company.

Die Verlagerung des Sitzes von ImageNet in Oklahoma von der unteren Ebene einer Garage in den neuen Sitz sowie die Verwendung von Plastik und Acryl ermöglichten es, ein neues Corporate Image zu schaffen. Das Unternehmen zeigt sich nun effizient, modern, schnell und professionell. Die Verlagerung des Firmensitzes und das neue Unternehmensimage machten es möglich, dass ImageNet den wichtigsten Vertrag zeichnen konnte, den es jemals im Werdegang des Unternehmens gab.

El traslado de la sede de ImageNet en Oklahoma desde el nivel inferior de un garaje a su nueva localización y el uso de materiales plásticos y acrílicos permitieron renovar la imagen de la compañía, convirtiéndola en la actualidad en una empresa que transmite eficiencia, modernidad, rapidez y profesionalidad. El cambio de sede y la renovación de su imagen permitieron a ImageNet firmar el mayor contrato en la historia de la empresa.

Le déménagement du siège d'ImageNet en Oklahoma du niveau inférieur d'un garage à son nouvel emplacement et le recours aux matériaux plastiques et acryliques ont permis de rénover l'image de la compagnie pour la convertir aujourd'hui en une entreprise faisant rimer efficacité, modernité, rapidité et professionnalisme. Le changement de siège et la rénovation de son image ont permis à ImageNet de signer le plus gros contrat de l'histoire de la société.

Il trasferimento della sede d'ImageNet in Oklahoma dal piano interrato di un garage alla sua nuova ubicazione, e l'uso di materiali plastici ed acrilici, ha permesso di rinnovare l'immagine della ditta che trasmette efficienza, modernità, rapidità e professionalità. La nuova sede e la sua nuova immagine hanno permesso ad ImageNet di firmare il contratto più importante della sua storia.

Our History

BMI Systems was
incorporated in 1977,
and the business
originated in 1956 as a
small, one man
typewriter repair shop
called Southwest
Typewriter Company.
Bobby Roberson
started this company
from his garage in
South Oklahoma City.
Today BMI Systems and
its affiliates, employ
over 400 people in
eleven cities and five
states.

GIOVANNITTI/DAVID GIOVANNITTI & PHILIP KERZNER | NEW YORK
NORMAN JAFFE. ROMANTIC MODERNIST
Parrish Art Museum, Southampton, NY, USA | 2005

The Plexiglas panels were designed specifically for the exhibition about the architect Norman Jaffe, orga-
nized by the Parrish Art Museum of Southampton. The translucent panels highlight the exhibited laminates and photographs and they can also be adapted to the needs and space available in each of the
rooms of the museum.

Die Plexiglaspaneele der Bilder wurden eigens für eine Ausstellung über den Architekten Norman Jaffe entworfen, die vom Parrish Art Museum in Southampton organisiert wurde. Die lichtdurchlässigen Paneele
überlassen den ausgestellten Bildern und Fotografien die Hauptrolle. Sie ermöglichen verschiedene Anord-
nungen und sind so immer an die räumlichen Anforderungen in jedem Saal des Museums anpassbar.

Los paneles de plexiglás de las imágenes fueron diseñados expresamente para la exposición sobre el arquitecto Norman Jaffe organizada por el Parrish Art Museum de Southampton. Los paneles, translúcidos,
ceden todo el protagonismo a las láminas y fotografías expuestas y permiten diversas configuraciones,
adaptándose a las necesidades y al espacio disponible en cada una de las salas del museo.

Les panneaux de plexiglas des images ont été conçus expressément pour l'exposition sur l'architecte
Norman Jaffe organisée par le Parrish Art Museum de Southampton. Les panneaux, translucides, cèdent
la vedette aux illustrations et photographies exposées et permettent diverses configurations en s'adap-
tant aux besoins et à l'espace disponible dans chacune des salles du musée.

I pannelli in plexiglas delle immagini, sono stati disegnati espressamente per la mostra sull'architetto Norman Jaffe, organizzata dal Parrish Art Museum di Southampton. I pannelli, translucidi, cedono tutto il protagonismo ai disegni ed alle foto esposte, consentendo varie configurazioni che si adattano alle necessità ed allo spazio disponibile in ogni sala del museo.

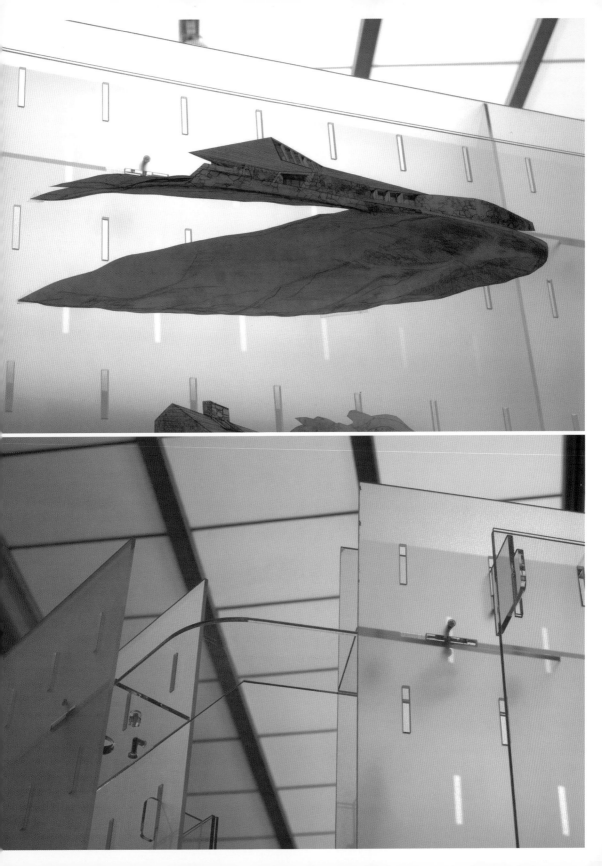

One of the two structures of this house in Tijuana (the white one) is covered with polycarbonate laminates. This material enhances the luminosity in the dwelling and gives it an altogether lighter feel. Another of the benefits of polycarbonate is that it is very easy to clean. In this case a watering system fitted in the roof allows it to be cleaned solely with water. Moreover, the polycarbonate covering can be replaced, when necessary, by another in a different color or with a different level of transparency.

Einer der beiden Körper dieses Hauses in Tijuana (der Weiße) ist mit Polykarbonat verkleidet. Das Polykarbonat lässt Licht in das Innere des Hauses fallen, wodurch das Gebäude visuell leichter wirkt. Ein anderer Vorteil dieses Materials ist die einfache Reinigung. In diesem Fall wurde ein Bewässerungssystem auf dem Dach montiert, das eine einfache Reinigung mit Wasser ohne Zusätze ermöglicht. Die Verkleidung aus Polykarbonat kann auch jederzeit problemlos durch eine andere in einer anderen Farbe oder mit mehr oder weniger Transparenz ersetzt werden.

Uno de los dos volúmenes de esta vivienda de Tijuana (el blanco) cuenta con un revestimiento de láminas de policarbonato. El policarbonato permite la entrada de la luz y aligera visualmente la casa. Otra de las ventajas del policarbonato es que resulta muy fácil de limpiar. En este caso, un sistema de riego instalado en el techo permite limpiarlo utilizando únicamente agua. El revestimiento de policarbonato, además, puede ser reemplazado sin problemas y en cualquier momento por otro de un color o grado de transparencia distinto.

L'un des deux volumes de cette demeure de Tijuana (le blanc) compte un revêtement de feuilles de polycarbonate. Le polycarbonate laisse la lumière s'infiltrer à l'intérieur de la maison et l'allège visuellement. Autre avantage du polycarbonate : il est très facile à laver. En l'occurrence, un système d'arrosage installé sur le toit permet de le laver en utilisant uniquement de l'eau. Le revêtement de polycarbonate, peut, en outre, être remplacé sans problèmes par un autre d'une couleur ou d'un niveau de transparence distinct, à tout moment.

Uno dei due volumi di questa casa di Tijuana (il bianco) presenta un rivestimento di lamine di policarbonato. Il policarbonato permette l'ingresso della luce all'interno della casa alleggerendola visivamente. Altro vantaggio del policarbonato è la sua estrema facilità di pulizia. In questo caso, un sistema idraulico installato sul tetto consente di pulirlo con solo dell'acqua. Il rivestimento di policarbonato, inoltre, può essere sostituito in qualsiasi momento e senza problemi con un altro di un colore o grado di trasparenza diverso.

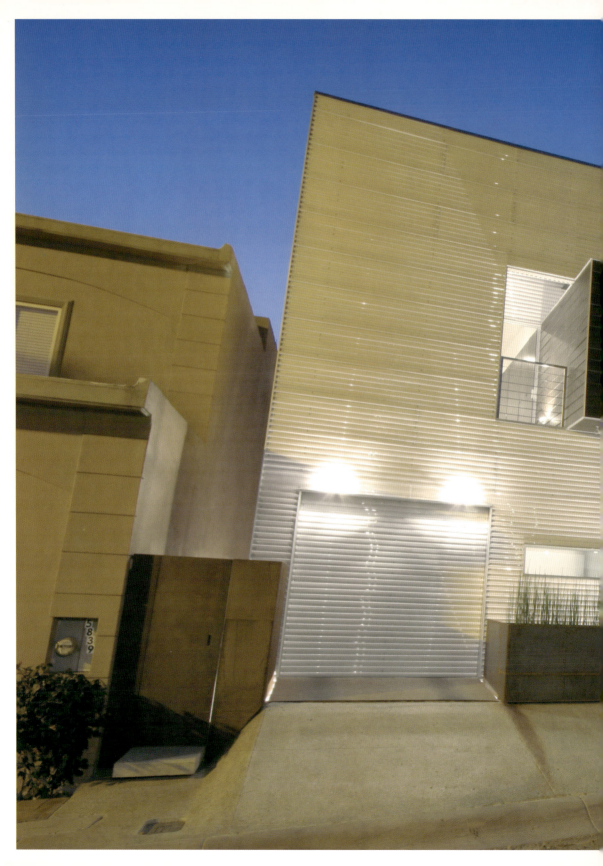

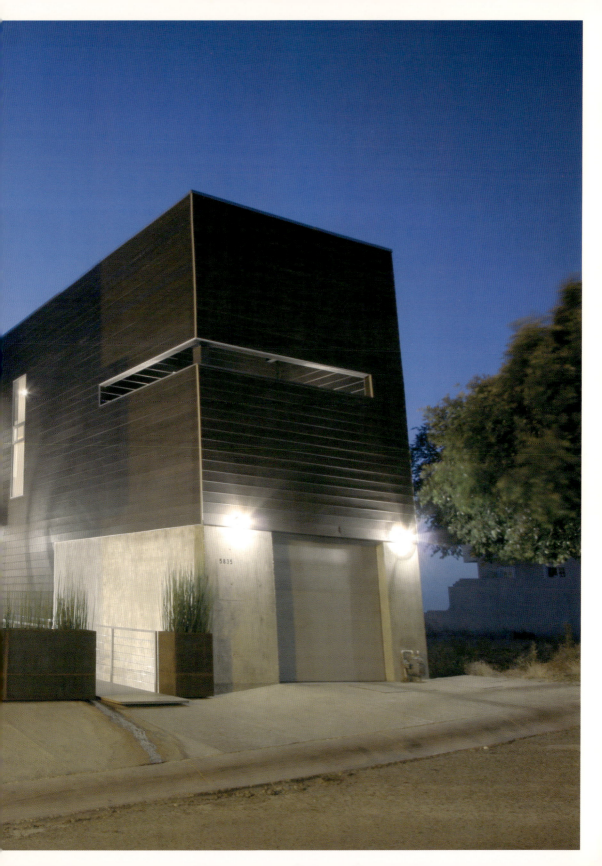

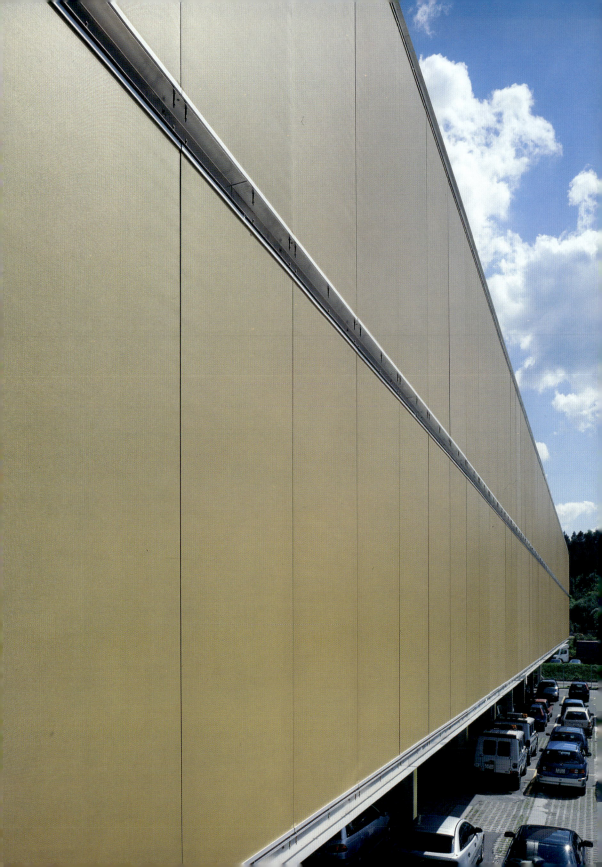

The plastic facade of this artworks warehouse surrounds the whole building and converts it into a continuous structure which detracts from the car park situated below. The warehouse opens a year to the public four times for young artists to exhibit their work in several of the rooms, thus transforming itself periodically into a gallery dedicated to young talent.

Die Kunststofffassade dieses Lagers für Kunstwerke umgibt das Gebäude vollständig und macht es zu einem durchgehenden Körper, dessen beeindruckende Präsenz den Parkplatz, der sich darunter befindet, unauffälliger macht. Das Lager wird viermal im Jahr für das Publikum geöffnet, damit junge Künstler ihre Werke in den verschiedenen Räumen ausstellen können. So wird es von Zeit zu Zeit zu einer Galerie für junge Talente.

La fachada de plástico de este almacén de obras de arte rodea por completo el edificio y lo convierte en un volumen continuo cuya impactante presencia difumina la del *parking* situado debajo. El almacén se abre cuatro veces al año al público para que artistas jóvenes expongan su obra en varias de sus estancias, convirtiéndose así periódicamente en una galería de jóvenes talentos.

La façade plastique de ce magasin d'œuvres d'art ceint l'ensemble de l'édifice et le convertit en un volume continu dont la présence saisissante gomme celle du parking situé juste en dessous. Le magasin s'ouvre quatre fois par an au public afin que les jeunes artistes exposent leur œuvre dans plusieurs de ses salles, le convertissant ainsi périodiquement en galerie pour les nouveaux talents.

La facciata di plastica di questo magazzino d'opere d'arte circonda completamente l'edificio, trasformandolo in un volume continuo, la sua forte presenza lenisce quella del parcheggio situato sotto. Il magazzino, che apre al pubblico quattro volte all'anno, per consentire ai giovani artisti di esporre le loro opere in varie sale, si trasforma periodicamente in una galleria di giovani talenti.

OQO is an oriental restaurant located in Islington Green which doubles up as a cocktail bar. The design – organic, minimalist and functional – combines a spectacular black granite bar with polycarbonate, silk and wood. The result is a colorful, contemporary space of sensual lines which transmits the quality of simplicity and efficiency – a characteristic of the cuisine.

OQO ist ein orientalisches Restaurant in Islington Green, das gleichzeitig auch eine Cocktailbar ist. Innerhalb der organischen, minimalistischen und funktionellen Gestaltung wurde eine auffallende Bar aus schwarzem Granit mit Polykarbonat, Seide und Holz kombiniert. So entstand ein bunter, zeitgemäßer Raum mit gefühlvollen Linien, der die Idee von Einfachheit und Schnelligkeit vermittelt. Auch die Gerichte, die hier zubereitet werden, entsprechen dieser Linie.

OQO es un restaurante oriental localizado en Islington Green que funciona también como *cocktail bar*. El diseño, orgánico, minimalista y funcional, combina una espectacular barra de granito negro con el policarbonato, la seda y la madera. El resultado es un espacio colorido, contemporáneo y de líneas sensuales que transmite la idea de simplicidad y rapidez que caracteriza su cocina.

OQO est un restaurant oriental situé à Islington Green faisant également office de bar. Le design organique, minimaliste et fonctionnel combine un spectaculaire comptoir de granit noir avec le polycarbonate, la soie et le bois. En résulte un espace coloriste, contemporain et aux lignes sensuelles qui transmet l'idée de simplicité et de rapidité caractéristique de sa cuisine.

OQO è un ristorante orientale ubicato ad Islington Green che funge anche da *cocktail bar*. Il disegno, organico, minimalista e funzionale, abbina uno spettacolare bancone di granito nero al policarbonato, la seta ed il legno. Il risultato è uno spazio colorista, contemporaneo, dalle linee sensuali che trasmette l'idea di semplicità e rapidità, qualità che caratterizzano la sua cucina.

The back lighting of the polycarbonate panels of the facade of this cultural center of Dalston, Hackney, can be easily replaced, which allows for changes of color and hence the ambience of the structure. The building which follows a clearly European model and which was designed as a sprinboard for the rehabilitation of the area, houses a center for community resources, a small business center and a space for cultural activities.

Die Beleuchtung hinter den Polykarbonatpaneelen der Fassade dieses Kulturzentrums in Dalston, Hackney, kann einfach ausgetauscht werden, so dass man die Farbe und die Wirkung verändern kann. Das Gebäude ist in einem eindeutig europäischen Stil gestaltet. Es handelt sich um ein Pilotprojekt für die Sanierung des Stadtteils, in dem es sich befindet, und beherbergt ein Zentrum mit Installationen für die Gemeinschaft, ein kleines Geschäftszentrum und einen Raum für kulturelle Aktivitäten.

Las luces que iluminan por detrás los paneles de policarbonato de la fachada de este centro cultural de Dalston, Hackney, pueden ser reemplazadas fácilmente, lo que permite cambiar el color y la atmósfera del volumen. El edificio, que sigue un modelo claramente europeo y que fue diseñado como punta de lanza de la rehabilitación del área en la que se encuentra, alberga un centro de recursos para la comunidad, un pequeño centro de negocios y un espacio para actividades culturales.

Les lumières qui éclairent par derrière les panneaux de polycarbonate de la façade de ce centre culturel de Dalston, Hackney, peuvent être facilement remplacées, ce qui permet de modifier la couleur et l'atmosphère du volume. L'édifice, qui suit un modèle clairement européen et fut conçu comme fer de lance de la réhabilitation de la zone, accueille un centre de ressources pour la communauté, un petit centre d'affaires et un espace d'activités culturelles.

Le luci che illuminano da dietro i pannelli di policarbonato della facciata di questo centro culturale di Dalston, Hackney, sono facilmente sostituibili, cosa che consente di cambiare il colore e l'atmosfera del volume. L'edificio, che segue un modello chiaramente europeo, e che è stato disegnato come esempio della riabilitazione dell'area in cui si trova, accoglie un centro di risorse per la comunità, un piccolo centro d'affari ed uno spazio per attività culturali.

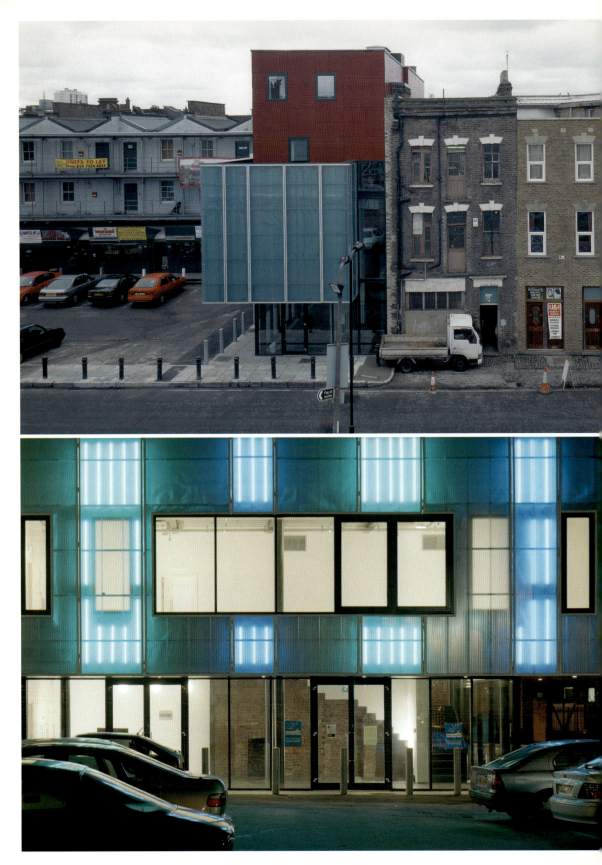

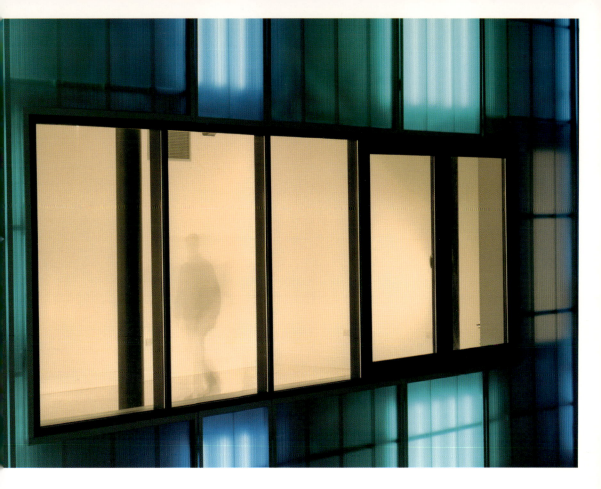

The back wall of this sauna (which is also a greenhouse) was covered with polycarbonate panels. Behind the panels the different colored fluorescent tubes which illuminate the structure are visible. The facade of the greenhouse also uses polycarbonate panels which are behind the glass windows.

Die Rückwand dieser Sauna, die gleichzeitig ein Gewächshaus ist, wurde mit Polykarbonatpaneelen verkleidet. Hinter diesen Paneelen sitzen Leuchtstoffröhren in verschiedenen Farben, die diesen Teil des Gebäudes beleuchten. Auch im Gewächshaus verwendete man Polykarbonatpaneele, und zwar an der Fassade hinter den Glasscheiben.

La pared trasera de esta sauna –que es a la vez un invernadero– ha sido recubierta con paneles de policarbonato. Tras los paneles, pueden observarse los tubos fluorescentes de diferentes colores que iluminan el volumen. También en el invernadero se han utilizado paneles de policarbonato, concretamente en la fachada, detrás del vidrio de los ventanales.

La paroi arrière de ce sauna (qui sert également de jardin d'hiver) a été recouverte de panneaux de polycarbonate. Il est loisible d'observer, derrière les panneaux, les tubes fluorescents de différentes couleurs qui illuminent le volume. Le jardin d'hiver a également vu l'utilisation de panneaux de polycarbonate, concrètement pour la façade, derrière le verre du fenêtrage.

La parete posteriore di questa sauna –che funge anche da serra– è stata ricoperta con pannelli di policarbonato. Dietro i pannelli, vi sono i tubi fluorescenti di vari colori che illuminano il volume. Nella serra sono stati impiegati pannelli di policarbonato, soprattutto sulla facciata, dietro il vetro dei finestroni.

It is a shop selling photographic, optical and electronic products. Its facade was covered with opaque poly-carbonate panels (blue on the back) during the renovation, which led to the construction of a completely new building where the lower level is for sales to the public and upstairs for offices and storage.

Ein Geschäft für fotografische, optische und elektronische Produkte. Die Fassade wurde mit lichtundurch-lässigen Polykarbonatpaneelen verkleidet, deren Rückseiten blau sind. Die Renovierung dieses Gebäudes bedeutete praktisch einen Neubau, in dem sich die Verkaufsräume auf der unteren Ebene und die Büros und Lagerräume im Obergeschoss befinden.

Una tienda de productos de fotografía, óptica y electrónica. Su fachada fue recubierta con opacos pane-les de policarbonato –de color azul por su parte trasera– durante su reforma, que supuso la construc-ción de un edificio completamente nuevo, en el que el nivel inferior se reservó para el espacio de venta al público y el superior, para oficinas y almacenamiento.

Une boutique de produits de photographie, optique et électronique. Sa façade a été recouverte de pan-neaux de polycarbonate opaques (de couleur bleue pour sa partie arrière) lors de sa réforme, impliquée par la construction d'un édifice complètement neuf où le niveau inférieur a été réservé à l'espace de vente au public et le supérieur pour les bureaux et l'entreposage.

Questo è un negozio di prodotti per fotografia, ottica ed elettronica. Durante la ristrutturazione, che ha implicato la costruzione di un edificio completamente nuovo, la facciata è stata ricoperta con pannelli di policarbonato opachi –blu dalla parte posteriore–. Il piano inferiore è stato riservato allo spazio di vendi-ta al pubblico e quello superiore agli uffici e magazzino.

The project Terminal V involved the creation of offices for 20 people and its most outstanding feature is the curved facade made from fiber glass which resembles an airplane. Inside, the light system has been concealed in order to create a soft light which diffuses the edges and reduces the impact of the lighting in the interior design.

Was zuerst an diesem Bauprojekt Terminal V, einem Bürogebäude für zwanzig Personen, auffällt, ist die kurvenförmige Fassade aus Glasfaser, die deutlich an ein Flugzeug erinnert. Im Inneren des Gebäudes wurden die Lampen verborgen angebracht, um so eine indirekte Beleuchtung zu schaffen, die die Umrisse verwischt und es vermeidet, dass eine Lichtquelle eine zu wichtige Rolle in der Innendekoration einnimmt.

Lo primero que llama la atención del proyecto Terminal V, unas oficinas con capacidad para veinte personas, es su fachada de formas curvas, fabricada en fibra de vidrio y que recuerda claramente a un avión. En el interior del edificio las luminarias han sido ocultadas a la vista del público con el objeto de crear una iluminación matizada que difumine los contornos y para evitar que los puntos de luz se conviertan en protagonistas de la decoración interior.

La façade du projet Terminal V, des bureaux d'une capacité de 20 personnes, est le premier élément attirant l'attention avec ses formes courbes, fabriquées en fibre de verre et rappelant clairement un avion. À l'intérieur de l'édifice, les luminaires ont été occultés de la vue du public afin de créer un éclairage nuancé qui estompe les contours et pour éviter que les points de lumière ne prennent la vedette dans le décor intérieur.

La prima cosa che colpisce del progetto Terminal V, degli uffici con capienza per venti persone, è la facciata dalle forme ricurve, fabbricata in fibra di vetro e che ricorda chiaramente un aereo. All'interno dell'edificio le luci sono state nascoste alla vista del pubblico per creare un'illuminazione sfumata che attenua i contorni, e per evitare che i punti luce siano i protagonisti della decorazione interna.

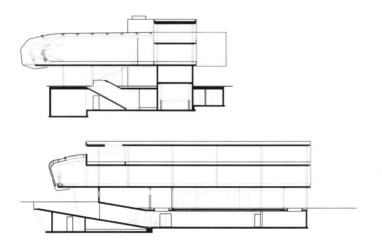

The circular acrylic brackets hang from the roof so that the glasses on show appear to be floating over a human face. The fitted zenithal spot lights are reflected in each of the brackets through the groove creating an almost ghostly effect similar to that of weightlessness. The objective was to create a pleasant and attractive space, visually light, which resulted in the use of plastic in the interior design.

Die kreisförmigen Konsolen aus Acryl, die man auf den Bildern sieht, hängen an der Decke und erwecken so den Eindruck, dass die ausgestellten Brillen über einem menschlichen Antlitz schweben. Das Licht, das von den Scheinwerfern stammt, die in die Decke eingebaut sind, wird auf jeder der Konsolen über die Rillen reflektiert, was sie fast geisterhaft schwerelos wirken lässt. Ziel war es, einen angenehmen und einladenden, visuell leichten Raum zu schaffen. Deshalb entschied man sich für Kunststoffmaterialien bei der Innengestaltung.

Las repisas circulares acrílicas que pueden verse en las imágenes cuelgan del techo para crear la sensación de que las gafas expuestas flotan sobre una cara humana. La luz de los focos cenitales empotrados en el techo se refleja en cada una de las repisas a través de las ranuras, provocando un efecto casi fantasmal, similar a la ingravidez. El objetivo fue crear un espacio agradable y amable, visualmente liviano, y de ahí el uso de materiales plásticos en su interiorismo.

Les étagères circulaires acryliques visibles sur les images pendent du plafond pour créer la sensation que les lunettes exposées flottent sur un visage humain. La lumière des spots zénithaux encastrés au plafond se reflète sur chaque marche à travers les rainures en provoquant un effet presque fantasmatique similaire à l'apesanteur. L'objectif était de créer un espace agréable et plaisant, léger visuellement, de là le recours aux matières plastiques pour ses intérieurs.

I ripiani circolari acrilici, visibili nelle immagini che pendono dal tetto, servono a creare la sensazione che gli occhiali esposti fluttuino su di un volto umano. La luce degli spot incassati sul soffitto si riflette su ognuno dei ripiani attraverso le scanalature, provocando un effetto quasi irreale simile all'assenza di gravità. L'obiettivo era quello di creare uno spazio gradevole e piacevole, visivamente etereo, che giustifica l'uso dei materiali plastici nel suo interno.

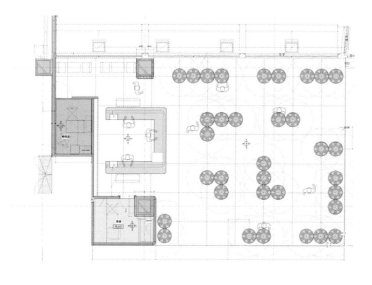

IVAN KROUPA ARCHITECTS | PRAGUE
BB CENTRE RECEPTION
Prague, Czech Republic | 1999

The opaque Perspex (PMMA) laminas which frame the reception area of this administrative building appear to be levitating between the ceiling and the floor. Each one of them boasts its own unique light source. The layout of the laminas which results in an interesting play on light and colors and the different light fittings make the space dynamic, converting it into an oasis of color in the midst of the coldness of the building in which it is housed.

Die lichtundurchlässigen Plexiglasleisten (PMMA), die die Rezeption in diesem Verwaltungsgebäude umrahmen, scheinen zwischen dem Boden und der Decke zu schweben. Jede von ihnen verfügt über eine eigene Lichtquelle, die sich von der anderen Leisten unterscheidet. Das Spiel mit Licht und Farben, das durch diese eigenwillig Verteilung der Leisten und verschiedenen Beleuchtungskörper entsteht, lässt den Raum dynamisch wirken und macht ihn zu einer Insel der Farben inmitten des kalten Gebäudes, in dem sie sich befindet.

Las láminas opacas de plexiglás (PMMA) que enmarcan la recepción de este edificio administrativo parecen levitar entre el pavimento y el techo. Cada una de ellas cuenta con una fuente de luz propia y diferente a las del resto de las láminas. El juego de luces y colores provocado por la caprichosa distribución de las láminas y las diferentes luminarias dinamiza el espacio, convirtiéndolo en una isla de color en medio de la frialdad del edificio en el que se encuentra.

Les feuilles opaques de perspex (PMMA) qui encadrent la réception de cet immeuble administratif semblent léviter entre le sol et le plafond. Chacune compte sa propre source de lumière distincte de celle des autres feuilles. Le jeu de lumières et de couleurs provoqué par la distribution capricieuse des feuilles et les différents luminaires dynamise l'espace, le convertissant en une île de couleur au milieu de la froideur de l'immeuble l'accueillant.

Le lamine opache di plexiglas (PMMA) che rifiniscono la reception di questo edificio amministrativo sembrano levitare tra il pavimento ed il tetto. Ognuna è dotata di una fonte di luce propria, diversa da quelle delle altre lamine. Il gioco di luce e colori provocato dalla capricciosa distribuzione delle lamine e le varie luminarie dinamizza lo spazio, trasformandolo in un'isola colorata nel bel mezzo della freddezza dell'edificio nel quale si trova.

JOHN FRIEDMAN-ALICE KIMM ARCHITECTS | LOS ANGELES
CLUB SUGAR
Santa Monica, USA | 1999

In search of a space in which to see and be seen, where the communication was fluid and where (in the words of the architects themselves), a «sexually charged» atmosphere was paramount, plastic was chosen. This was due to it being a flexible and transparent material which allows the interesting use of textures, color distortions, reflections and different shapes. In this case the hard plastic surfaces were balanced with very different materials: the bricks of one of the walls and the wooden roof structure.

Es sollte ein Raum geschaffen werden, in dem man sehen kann und gesehen wird, in dem die Kommunikation fließt und in dem, in den Worten des Architekten, eine „sexuell beeinflusste" Atmosphäre herrschen soll. So entschied man sich für Kunststoff, ein flexibles und transparentes Material, das es ermöglicht, mit verschiedenen Texturen, Verzerrungen, Farben, Reflexen und Formen zu spielen. In diesem Fall wurden die harten Oberflächen des Kunststoffs durch Materialien mit gegenteiligen Eigenschaften ausgeglichen, wie z. B. dem Ziegelstein an einer der Wände und der Holzstruktur der Decke.

Con el objeto de crear un espacio en el que ver y ser visto, en el que la comunicación fuera fluida y en el que reinara una atmósfera «sexualmente cargada» (en palabras de los mismos arquitectos) se recurrió al plástico, un material flexible y transparente que permite jugar con texturas, distorsiones, colores, reflejos y formas diferentes. En este caso, las duras superficies de plástico se han equilibrado por medio de materiales de personalidad marcadamente diferente: los ladrillos de una de las paredes o la estructura de madera de la cubierta, por ejemplo.

Dans l'objectif de créer un espace où voir et être vu, où la communication serait fluide et où régnerait une atmosphère « sexuellement chargée » (les propres paroles des architectes), le plastique a été retenu comme matériau flexible et transparent permettant de jouer avec les différentes textures, distorsions de couleurs, reflets et formes. En l'occurrence, les superficies dures du plastique ont été compensées au moyen de matériaux à la personnalité radicalement différente : les briques de certains murs ou la structure en bois de la couverte, par exemple.

Con l'obiettivo di creare uno spazio in cui vedere ed essere visto, in cui la comunicazione fosse fluida ed in cui potesse regnare un'atmosfera «sessualmente carica» (secondo le parole degli architetti) si è ricorsi alla plastica, un materiale flessibile e trasparente che consente di giocare con le consistenze, distorsioni, colori, riflessi e forme diverse. In questo caso, le superfici dure della plastica sono state equilibrate con dei materiali dalla personalità marcatamente diversa come i mattoni di una delle pareti, o la struttura del legno della copertura, per esempio.

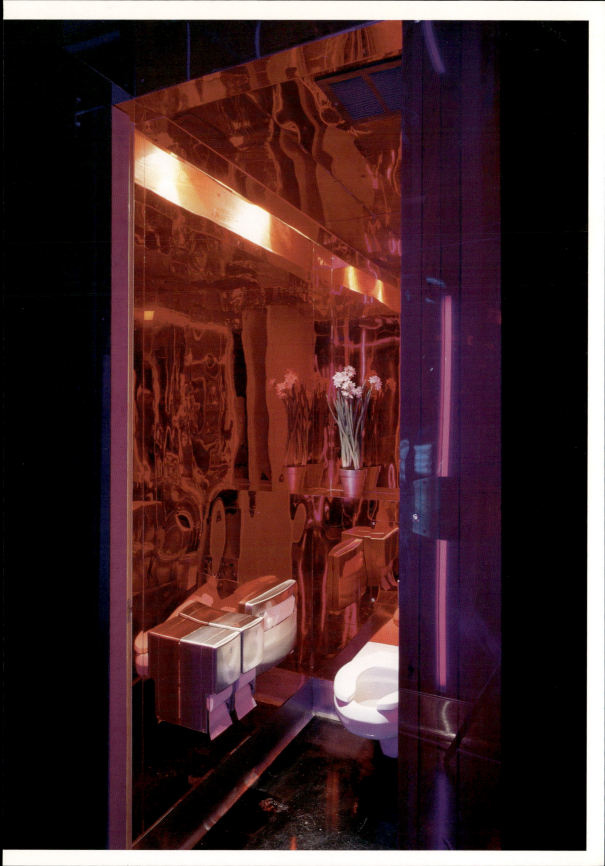

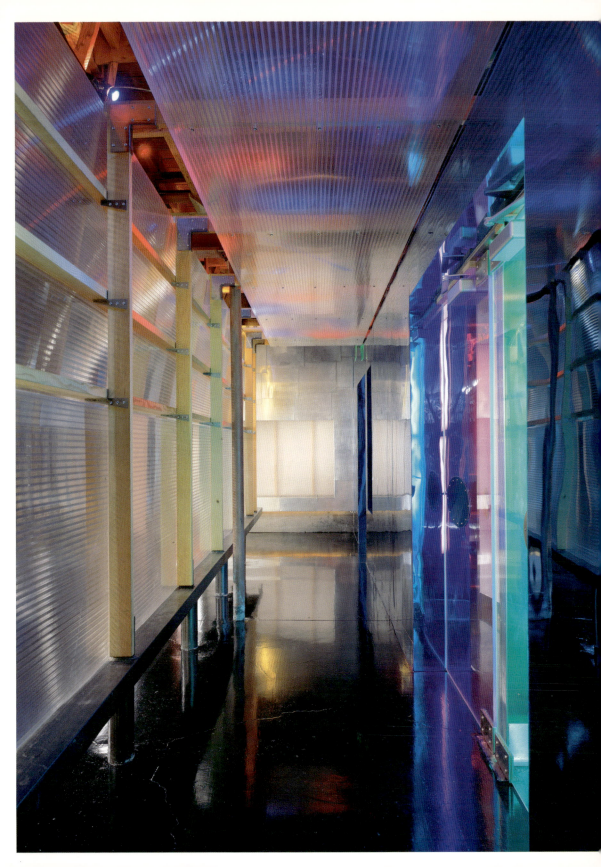

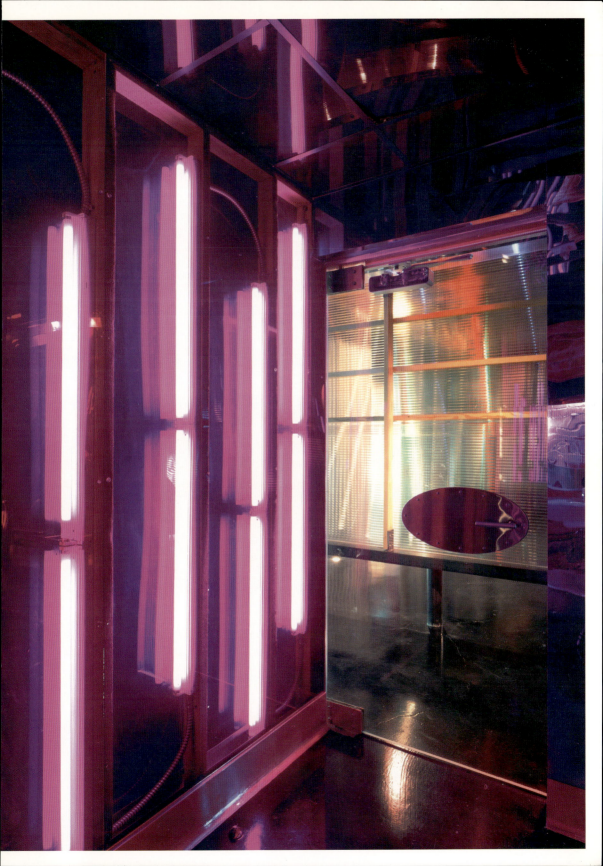

JOHN FRIEDMAN-ALICE KIMM ARCHITECTS | LOS ANGELES
L.A. DESIGN CENTER PHASE 1
Los Angeles, USA | 2003

Located in the neighborhood of South Central Los Angeles, the L.A. Design Center has been converted into the epicenter of the revitalization of the zone where several furniture manufacturers are concentrated. The variety of materials used in its restoration of which one was plastic, transmits the concept of integration, flexibility and transformation which is the basis of the activities of the center. The polycarbonate panels and acrylic materials used can be seen in both the exterior and the interior. The polycarbonate panel which covers the main facade of the building was designed to serve as a cinema screen on which to project images related to the activities of the center.

Das L.A. Design Center in South Central Los Angeles ist zu einem Epizentrum geworden, das dem Viertel neues Leben gibt. In diesen Räumen stellen zahlreiche Möbelhersteller ihre Produkte aus. Die Verschiedenartigkeit der Materialien, die bei dem Umbau benutzt wurden, unter anderem auch Kunststoff, vermittelt die Idee von Integration, Flexibilität und Umformung, die auch die Aktivitäten in diesem Zentrum prägt. Sowohl außen als auch innen wurden Polykarbonatpaneele und Materialien aus Acryl benutzt. Das Polykarbonatpaneel an der Vorderfassade des Gebäudes soll als eine Art Kinoleinwand dienen, auf die man Bilder projizieren kann, die mit den Aktivitäten des Zentrums im Zusammenhang stehen.

Localizado en el vecindario de South Central Los Angeles, el L.A. Design Center se ha convertido en el epicentro de la revitalización del barrio, un área en la que se concentran decenas de fabricantes de muebles. La variedad de materiales utilizados en su reforma, entre ellos el plástico, transmite la idea de integración, flexibilidad y transformación que preside la actividad del centro. Tanto en el exterior como en su interior podemos observar los paneles de policarbonato y los materiales acrílicos utilizados. El panel de policarbonato de la fachada frontal del edificio ha sido pensado para funcionar como pantalla de cine en la que proyectar imágenes relacionadas con la actividad del centro.

Situé dans le district de South Central à Los Angeles, le L.A. Design Center s'est converti en l'épicentre de la revitalisation du quartier, une zone où se concentrent des dizaines de fabricants de meubles. La variété des matériaux utilisés pour sa réforme, notamment le plastique, transmet l'idée d'intégration, de flexibilité et de transformation qui préside à l'activité du centre. À l'extérieur comme à l'intérieur, nous pouvons observer les panneaux de polycarbonate et les matériaux acryliques employés. Le panneau de polycarbonate visible dans la façade avant de l'édifice a été pensé pour fonctionner comme écran de cinéma où projeter des images liées à l'activité du centre.

Situato nella zona South Central Los Angeles, il L.A. Design Center è diventato l'epicentro della rinascita del quartiere, una zona in cui si concentrano decine di fabbricanti di mobili. La varietà dei materiali usati nella sua ristrutturazione, tra i quali la plastica, da un'idea d'integrazione, flessibilità e trasformazione che presiede l'attività del centro. Tanto all'esterno quanto all'interno si possono osservare dei pannelli di policarbonato ed i materiali acrilici usati. Il pannello di policarbonato della facciata frontale dell'edificio è stato concepito come schermo da cinema sul quale proiettare le immagini relative all'attività del centro.

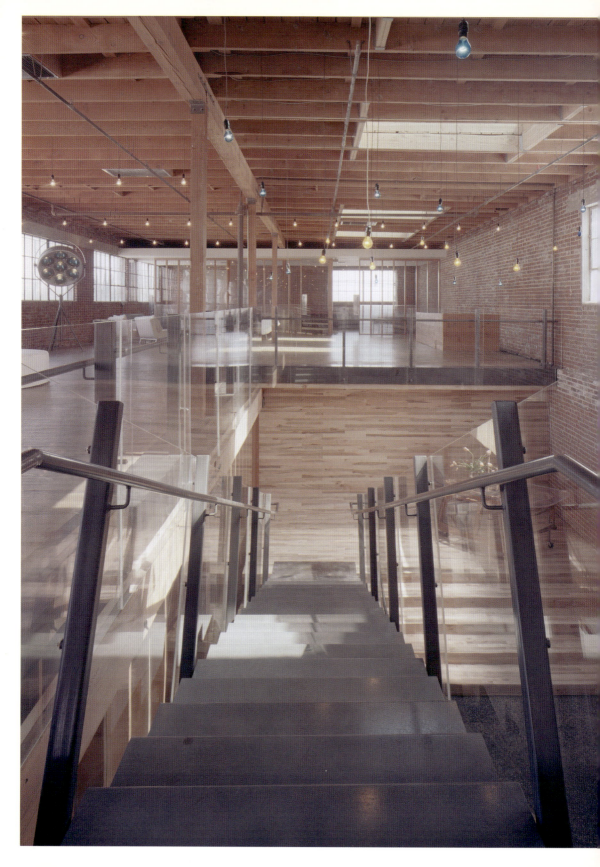

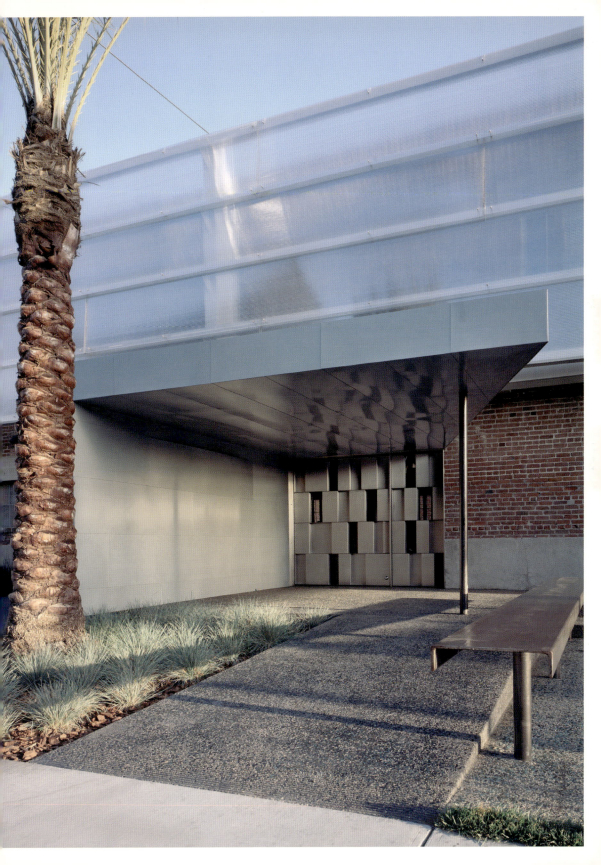

JOHN FRIEDMAN-ALICE KIMM ARCHITECTS | LOS ANGELES
THE BRIG
Los Angeles, USA | 2001

The owners of The Brig, a 58 year old bar located in Abbot Kinney Boulevard (Venice, Los Angeles), not only wanted to modernize the bar but also wanted it to contribute to the revitalization of the zone, thus becoming the heart of the social life of the neighborhood. Plastic was one of the most important materials in its alteration – apparent in the roof panels above the bar and the entrance, in the laminas which cover the walls and of course in the dj cabin.

Die Eigentümer von The Brig, eine 58 Jahre alte Bar in Abbot Kinney Boulevard (Venice, Los Angeles) wollten das Lokal nicht einfach nur renovieren und neu gestalten, sondern auch, dass es sich in das Viertel einfügt, ihm neues Leben gibt und zum Zentrum des sozialen Lebens im Viertel wird. Kunststoff ist eines der Materialien, das bei der Gestaltung dieser Räume am meisten benutzt wurde, und zwar als Deckenpaneele über der Bar und dem Eingang, als Leisten, die die Wände verkleiden und in der Kabine des DJs.

Los propietarios del The Brig, un bar de 58 años de antigüedad situado en Abbot Kinney Boulevard (Venice, Los Ángeles), no se conformaban simplemente con actualizar el local, sino que querían que éste se integrara y contribuyera a revitalizar el área, convirtiéndose en el centro de la vida social del barrio. El plástico es uno de los materiales más utilizados en su reforma: lo podemos encontrar en los paneles del techo sobre la barra y la entrada, en las láminas que revisten las paredes y, obviamente, en la cabina del *dj*.

Les propriétaires de The Brig, un bar affichant 58 ans d'ancienneté et situé sur Abbot Kinney Boulevard (Venice, Los Angeles), n'étaient pas satisfaits de la simple mise au goût du jour du lieu et souhaitaient plutôt qu'il s'intègre et contribue à revitaliser le quartier en le convertissant en centre de la vie sociale locale. Le plastique est l'un des matériaux les plus employés pour sa réforme : nous le retrouvons dans les panneaux du plafond au-dessus du comptoir et de l'entrée, dans les feuilles revêtant les parois et, bien entendu, dans la cabine du DJ.

I proprietari del The Brig, un bar aperto 58 anni fa, situato ad Abbot Kinney Boulevard (Venice, Los Angeles), non si accontentavano solo di ammodernare il locare, ma volevano che integrasse e contribuisse a ridare vita alla zona, diventando il centro della vita sociale del quartiere. La plastica è uno dei materiali più usati nella sua ristrutturazione: è presente nei pannelli del tetto sul bancone ed all'ingresso, nelle lamine di rivestimento delle pareti e, ovviamente, nella cabina del *dj*.

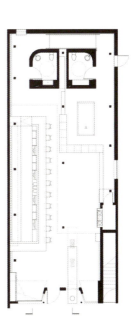

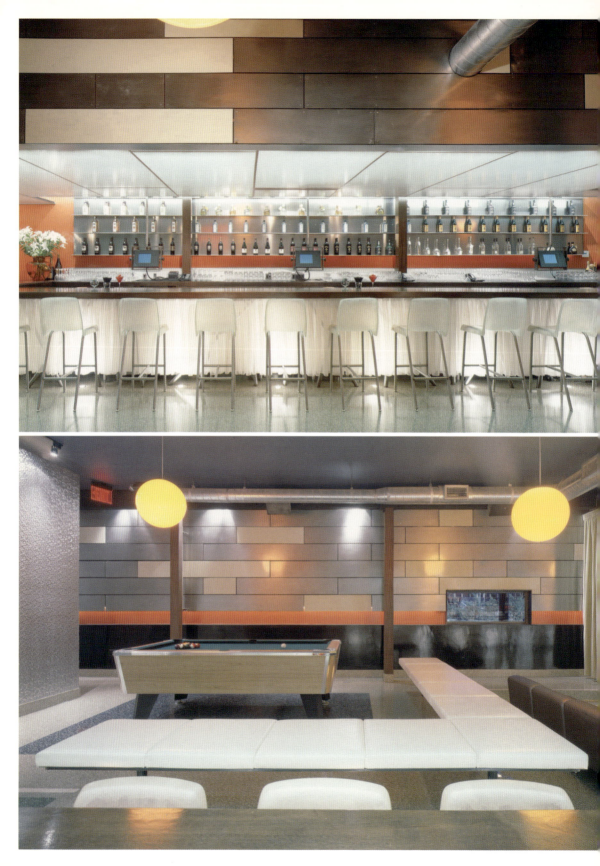

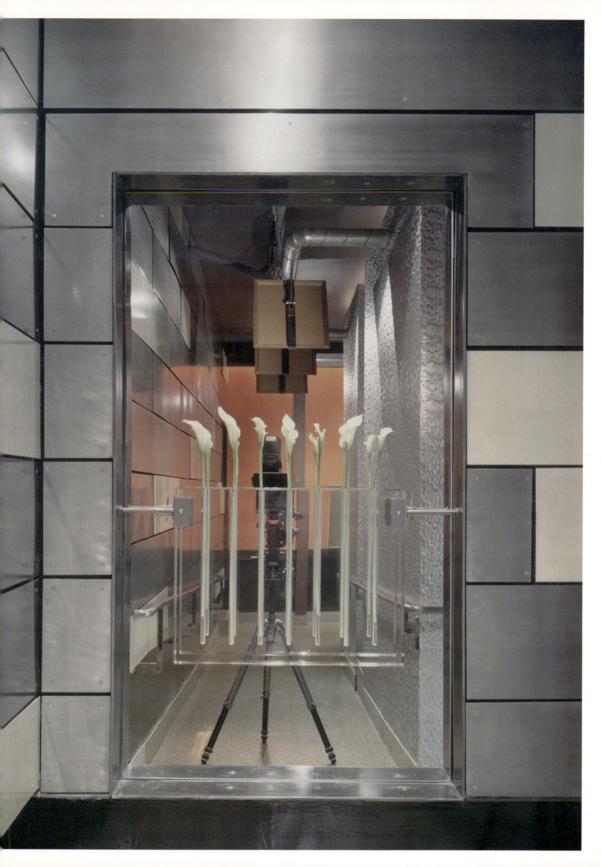

The epoxy plastic floor, the decorative wall features and the plastic lamps give this renowned bar-restaurant a contemporary ambience. It was launched in LA in 1931 and quickly became the place to be for celebrities from the world of cinema, music and art. However today the space undoubtedly emits the ultra-modern aesthetic of Canter's (its original 1953 premises), located in the old Esquire Theater in LA.

Der Boden aus Expoxyd, die Dekorationselemente an den Wänden und die Kunstofflampen dieses mythischen Bar-Restaurants, das ursprünglich in Los Angeles im Jahr 1931 eingeweiht wurde, und das schnell zu einem Treffpunkt für Persönlichkeiten aus der Welt des Kinos, der Musik und der Kunst wurde, lassen den Raum sehr modern wirken. Gleichzeitig wird jedoch an die ultramoderne Ästhetik des Canter's im Jahr 1953 erinnert, das sich im ehemaligen Esquire Theater in L.A. befand.

El suelo de plástico epoxídico, los elementos decorativos de las paredes y las lámparas, también de plástico, de este mítico bar-restaurante –cuyo enclave original, inaugurado en Los Ángeles en 1931, se convirtió rápidamente en lugar de encuentro de celebridades del mundo del cine, la música y el arte– confieren al espacio una atmósfera contemporánea que, sin embargo, remite inequívocamente a la estética ultra-moderna del Canter's de 1953, localizado en el viejo Esquire Theater de LA.

Le sol en plastique époxy, les éléments décoratifs des murs et les lampes, également en plastique, de ce bar-restaurant mythique dont l'enclave originelle, inaugurée à Los Angeles en 1931, s'est rapidement convertie en lieu de rencontre des célébrités du monde du cinéma, de la musique et des arts, confèrent à l'espace une atmosphère contemporaine qui, cependant, s'en remet sans équivoque à l'esthétique ultramoderne du Canter's de 1953, situé dans l'ancien Esquire Theater de LA.

Il pavimento plastico epossidico, gli elementi decorativi delle pareti e le lampade, anch'esse in plastica, di questo mitico bar-ristorante –la cui sede originale, inaugurata a Los Angeles nel 1931, divenne rapidamente il luogo d'incontro delle celebrità del mondo del cinema, della musica e dell'arte– conferiscono allo spazio un'atmosfera contemporanea che, però, rimanda senza dubbio all'estetica ultra moderna del Canter's del 1953, situato nel vecchio Esquire Theater di LA.

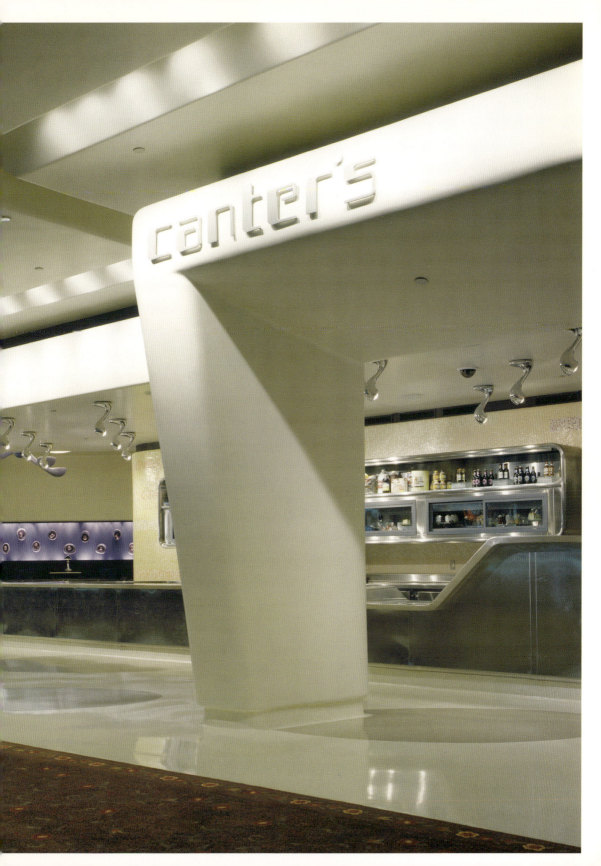

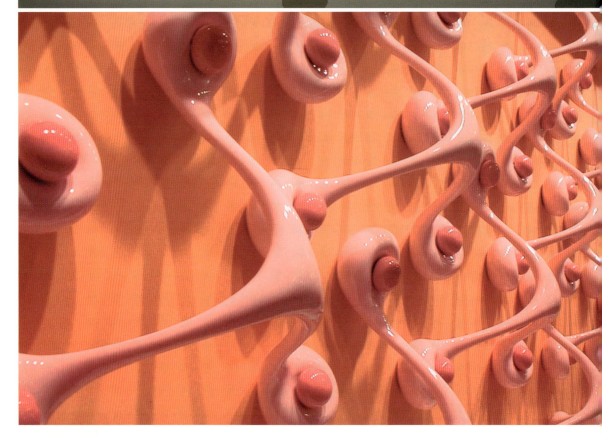

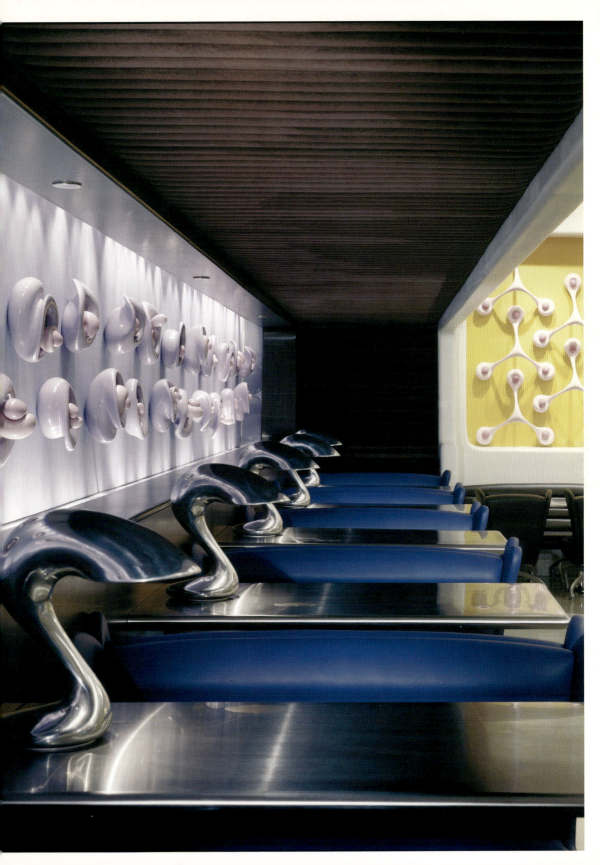

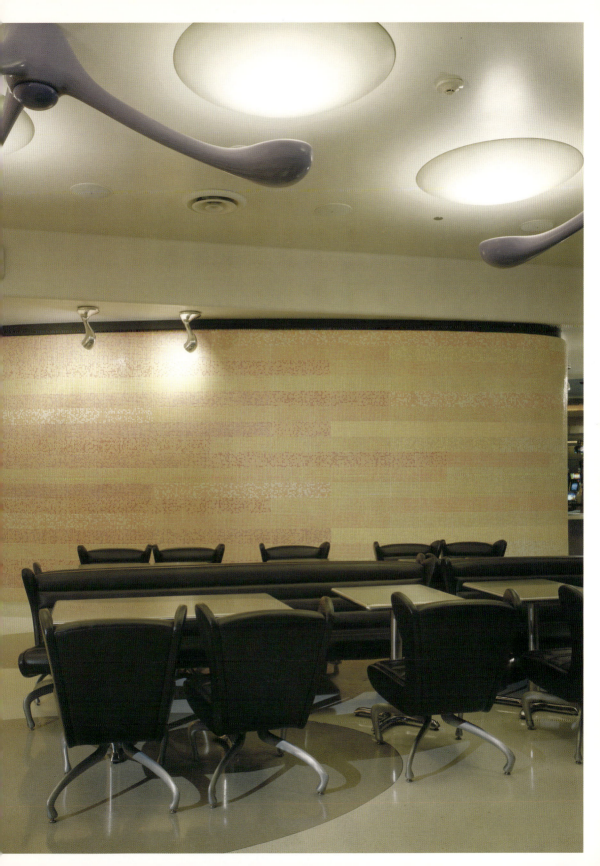

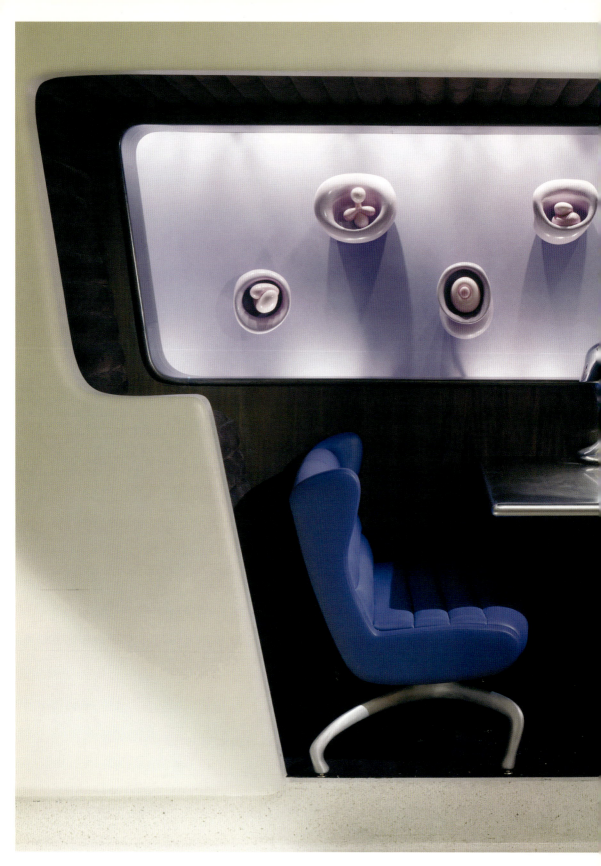

JORDAN MOZER & ASSOCIATES | CHICAGO
KARSTADT
Mülheim-Heissen, Germany | 2003

Plastic is the material which characterizes these large 4000 m^2 warehouses located near Dusseldorf. The walls, the floors, the organically shaped decorative panels and the illumination are made of plastic or materials made up of plastic and wood. The result is a space which clearly draws inspiration from the retro futuristic pop aesthetic of the 60's.

Kunststoff ist das Material, das dieses fast 4.000 Quadratmeter große Kaufhaus in einem Ort in der Nähe von Düsseldorf prägt und ihm Persönlichkeit verleiht. Sowohl am Boden als auch an den Wänden sind die dekorativen Paneele mit organischen Formen und die Beleuchtungskörper aus Kunststoff oder Verbundstoffen aus Kunststoff und Holz. Das Ergebnis ist ein Raum, der deutlich von der Pop-Art inspiriert ist und an die retrofuturistische Ästhetik der Sechzigerjahre erinnert.

El plástico es el material que caracteriza y confiere personalidad a estos grandes almacenes de casi 4.000 metros cuadrados, situados en una localidad cercana a Düsseldorf. Tanto el suelo como las paredes, los paneles decorativos de formas orgánicas y la iluminación son de plástico o de materiales compuestos de plástico y madera. El resultado es un espacio de clara inspiración pop que remite a la estética retrofuturista de los años sesenta.

Le plastique est le matériau qui caractérise et confère sa personnalité à ces grands magasins de près de 4 000 mètres carrés situés dans une ville proche de Düsseldorf. Pour le sol comme pour les parois, les panneaux décoratifs aux formes organiques et l'éclairage sont en plastique ou en matériaux composés de plastique et de bois. En résulte un espace à la claire inspiration pop qui rappelle l'esthétique rétrofuturiste des années 60.

La plastica è il materiale che caratterizza e personalizza questi grandi magazzini, di quasi 4.000 quadrati, situati in una località prossima a Düsseldorf. I pavimenti, le pareti, i pannelli decorativi dalla forme organiche, e l'illuminazione, sono di plastica o di materiali composti dalla plastica e legno. Il risultato è uno spazio di chiara ispirazione pop che richiama l'estetica retrofuturista degli anni sessanta.

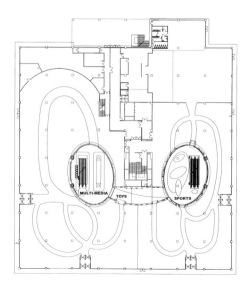

NECTAR
Las Vegas, USA | 2001

The curved organic shapes, the combination of colors and the overwhelming fantasy of the Chicago architect Jordan Mozer was enough to convince the owner of the Bellaggio hotel that he was the right person to carry out the design of Nector, one of the hotel's restaurants. With the aim of creating a glamorous, warm, comfortable and eye-catching space, Jordan Mozer used plastic in the floors, stools and cupboards. No other material would have been the source of such interesting use of shapes and colors.

Die organischen, gebogenen Formen, die wilden Farben und die sprühende Fantasie des Architekten Jordan Mozer reichten aus, um die Eigentümer des Hotels Bellaggio zu überzeugen, dass dieser Architekt aus Chicago die richtige Person war, um eines der Restaurants des Hotels, das Nectar, neu zu gestalten. Um eine glamouröse, warme, komfortable und auffallende Umgebung zu schaffen, verwendete Jordan Mozer Kunststoff an Böden, Hockern und Schränken. Kein anderes Material hätte das Spiel mit Formen und Farben in der Weise ermöglicht.

Las formas curvas de inspiración orgánica, el colorido desatado y la fantasía desbordante del arquitecto Jordan Mozer bastaron para convencer a los propietarios del hotel Bellaggio de que este arquitecto de Chicago era la persona adecuada para llevar a cabo el diseño de uno de los restaurantes del hotel, el Nectar. Con el objeto de crear un espacio glamuroso, cálido, confortable y llamativo, Jordan Mozer recurrió al plástico para los suelos, los taburetes y los armarios. Ningún otro material que no fuera el plástico hubiera permitido jugar con las formas y el colorido que puede verse en las fotos.

Les formes courbes d'inspiration organique, les coloris sauvages et la fantaisie débordante de l'architecte Jordan Mozer ont suffi pour convaincre les propriétaires de l'hôtel Bellaggio que cet architecte de Chicago était la personne idéale pour donner vie au design de l'un des restaurants de l'hôtel, le Nectar. Afin de créer un espace glamoureux, chaleureux, confortable et vivant, Jordan Mozer a retenu le plastique pour les sols, les tabourets et les armoires. Aucun autre matériau hormis le plastique n'aurait pu permettre de jouer avec les formes et les coloris comme l'illustrent les clichés.

Le forme curve d'ispirazione organica, il colore sfrenato e la debordante fantasia dell'architetto Jordan Mozer furono sufficienti a convincere i proprietari del hotel Bellaggio che questo architetto di Chicago fosse la persona giusta per realizzare il progetto del Nectar, uno dei ristoranti dell'albergo. Con l'idea di creare uno spazio con glamour, caldo, comodo e insolito, Jordan Mozer ha scelto la plastica per i pavimenti, gli sgabelli e gli armadi. Nessun altro materiale salvo la plastica può permettere di giocare con le forme e il colore come riportato nelle foto.

JORDI YAYA TUR-COLOCO DESIGN | BARCELONA
CLEAR
Barcelona, Spain | 2004

Plastics, synthetic and semi-synthetic polymer products are inexpensive, impermeable and above all ductile and easy to shape. This is what makes them perfect in the creation of a collection of round shaped furniture, with soft lines, reminiscent of the 60's, as in this hairdressing salon in the old town of Barcelona. In this way the computer screen is inset into the reception table and the clients' chairs are inset into the panel which holds the mirror in front of them.

Plastikmaterialien, Produkte aus synthetischen oder halbsynthetischen Polymeren, sind preisgünstig, wasserundurchlässig und vor allem dehnbar und einfach zu formen. Deshalb eignen sie sich ausgezeichnet dazu, Möbelgruppen mit rundlichen Formen, sanften Kanten und im Stil der Sechzigerjahre zu schaffen, wie man es in diesem Haarstudio in der Altstadt von Barcelona tat. Diese Möbel sind flexibel genug, um fugenlos einen Bildschirm an der Rezeption oder einen Stuhl für den Kunden in das Paneel, in dem sich der Spiegel dem Kunden gegenüber befindet, einzufügen.

Los plásticos, productos poliméricos sintéticos o semisintéticos, son baratos, impermeables y, sobre todo, dúctiles y fáciles de moldear. De ahí que resulten adecuados cuando, como en el caso de esta peluquería situada en el casco antiguo de Barcelona, se pretende crear una familia de muebles de formas redondeadas, contornos suaves y reminiscencias de los años sesenta, lo suficientemente flexibles como para integrar sin juntura alguna la pantalla del ordenador en la mesa de la recepción o la silla para los clientes en el panel que alberga el espejo frente a ella.

Les plastiques, produits polymères synthétiques ou semi synthétiques, sont économiques, imperméables et, surtout, ductiles et faciles à modeler. Pour ces raisons, ils sont appropriés lorsque, comme pour ce salon de coiffure du centre ancien de Barcelone, il s'agit de créer une famille de meubles aux formes arrondies, aux contours adoucis, réminiscences des années 60, et suffisamment flexibles pour intégrer sans raccord aucun l'écran d'un ordinateur dans la table de la réception, ou la chaise pour les clients dans le panneau accueillant le miroir lui faisant face.

I materiali plastici, prodotti polimerici sintetici o semisintetici, sono buon mercato, impermeabili e, soprattutto, duttili e facili da modellare. Ecco dunque che risultano essere idonei quando, come nel caso di questo parrucchiere situato nel centro storico di Barcellona, si vuole creare una famiglia di mobili dalle forme arrotondate, morbidi contorni e reminiscenze degli anni sessanta, sufficientemente flessibili per poter integrare senza giunture lo schermo del computer sul tavolo della reception, o la poltrona dei clienti nel pannello di fronte in cui è inserito lo specchio.

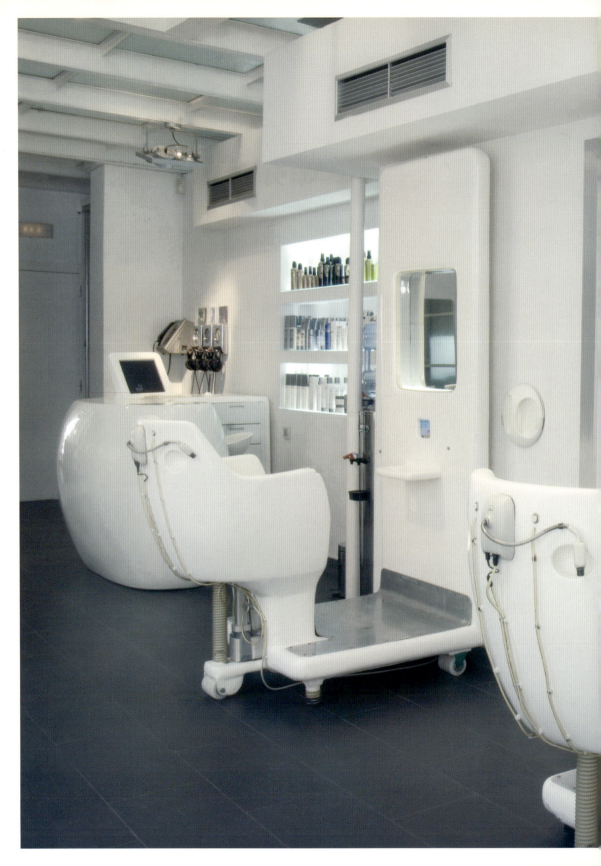

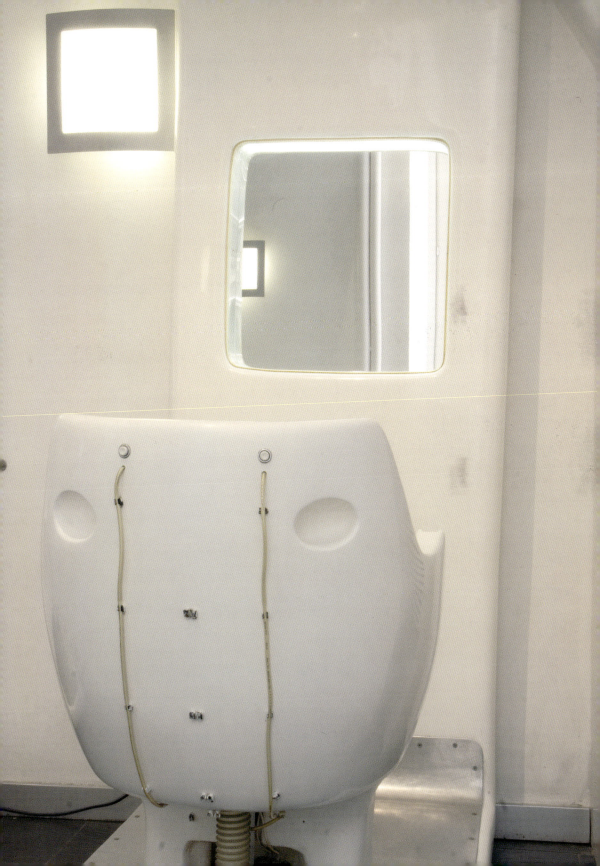

The idea of connecting the Aoyama and Stadium avenues using a fiber glass and reinforced plastic mesh covered with bamboo came about from the meetings and debates with the young workers of the NTT building. The idea was to give vitality back to an urban space considered overly rigid having been adapted to a 20th century urban plan. The mesh works as a capillary to be part of a hypothetical future network which will connect underdeveloped urban «holes».

In den Versammlungen und Diskussionen der jungen Arbeiter im Gebäude NTT Aoyama entstand die Idee, die Boulevards Aoyama und Stadium mit einem Netz aus Glas und Kunststoff zu verbinden, das mit einem Bambusdach verstärkt ist. Dadurch wollte man einen städtischen Raum neu beleben, den man als zu starr betrachtete, weil er auf hoffnungslose Weise an eine Stadtplanung aus dem 20. Jh. angepasst wurde. Das Netz stellt eine Art Gefäß innerhalb eines hypothetischen künftigen Netzes dar, das die urbanen „Löcher", die nicht wirklich genutzt werden, miteinander verbinden soll.

De las reuniones y debates con los jóvenes trabajadores del edificio NTT Aoyama surgió la idea de conectar las avenidas Aoyama y Stadium con una malla de fibra de vidrio y plástico reforzado cubierta con bambú. La idea era devolver la vitalidad a un espacio urbano considerado demasiado rígido, al haberse ajustado sin resquicios a una planificación urbanística propia del siglo XX. La malla actúa así como un capilar perteneciente a una hipotética futura red que conectaría «agujeros» urbanos desaprovechados.

Des réunions et débats avec les jeunes travailleurs de l'immeuble NTT Aoyama a surgi l'idée de connecter les avenues Aoyama et Stadium avec une maille de fibre de verre et de plastique renforcé dotée d'une couverte de bambou. L'idée était de rendre sa vitalité à un espace urbain considéré comme trop rigide après s'être ajusté très étroitement à une planification urbanistique propre du 20ème siècle. La maille agit comme un capillaire appartenant à un réseau hypothétique futur qui connecterait des « vides » urbains à l'abandon.

Dalle riunioni e dibattiti avuti con i giovani dipendenti dell'edificio NTT Aoyamo, è scaturita l'idea di collegare i viali Aoyama e Stadium con una maglia di fibra di vetro e plastica rinforzata ricoperta da bambù. L'idea mirava a ridare vitalità ad uno spazio urbano considerato troppo rigido, per aver sposato totalmente la pianificazione urbanistica tipica del XX secolo. La maglia funge così da capillare che appartiene ad un'ipotetica futura rete che collegherebbe i «vuoti» urbani non sfruttati.

This Chinese restaurant of approximately 185 m² occupies a typically New York space, which narrows in the central part as though it were the neck of a bottle, sandwiched between two glass roofs. Instead of bringing together the two spaces it was decided that they should have completely discordant personalities, in line with the rules of the game of the exquisite corpse, popularized by the surrealists. The acrylic corridor which connects the two spaces contains the bathroom and runs along the whole premises from the wall to the roof and then it drops and is integrated into the bar counter.

Dieses ungefähr 185 Quadratmeter große, chinesische Restaurant liegt in einem Gebäude, das sehr typisch für New York ist, schmal in der Mitte zwischen zwei Dachfenstern, und an einen Flaschenhals erinnernd. Anstatt die beiden Zonen ineinander zu integrieren, entschloss man sich dazu, ihnen einen ganz unterschiedlichen Charakter zu geben, wobei man sich von den Regeln des Spiels des Cadavre Exquis inspirieren ließ, das bei den Surrealisten so beliebt war. Der Flur aus Acrylmaterial, der die beiden Bereiche miteinander verbindet, enthält ein Bad und erstreckt sich an dem ganzen Lokal entlang, von der Wand bis zur Decke, dann sinkt er nach unten und integriert sich in die Bar.

Este restaurante chino de aproximadamente 185 metros cuadrados ocupa un espacio típicamente neoyorquino, que se estrecha en su parte central como si se tratara de un cuello de botella, emparedado entre dos lucernarios. En lugar de integrar los dos espacios se ha optado por darles una personalidad completamente discordante siguiendo las reglas del juego del cadáver exquisito popularizado por los surrealistas. El pasillo de material acrílico que conecta los dos espacios integra el cuarto de baño y se extiende a lo largo de todo el local, desde la pared hasta el techo, para luego bajar e integrarse en la barra del bar.

Ce restaurant chinois de près de 185 mètres carrés occupe un espace typiquement new-yorkais, s'étendant en son centre comme s'il s'agissait d'un col de bouteille, emmuré entre deux lucernaires. Au lieu d'intégrer les deux espaces, le choix a été fait de conférer une personnalité complètement discordante en suivant les règles du jeu des cadavres exquis, popularisé par les surréalistes. Le couloir en matière acrylique qui connecte les deux espaces intègre les toilettes et s'étend tout au long du local, du mur au plafond pour ensuite descendre et s'intégrer au comptoir du bar.

Questo ristorante cinese di circa 185 metri quadrati occupa uno spazio tipico di New York, che si restringe nella sua parte centrale come in un collo di bottiglia, ristretto tra due lucernai. Invece d'integrare i due spazi, si è scelto di dargli una personalità completamente discordante seguendo le regole del gioco del cadavere squisito reso popolare dai surrealisti. Il corridoio in materiale acrilico collega i due spazi con il bagno, stendendosi lungo tutto il locale, dalla parete sino al tetto, per poi scendere ed integrarsi nel bancone del bar.

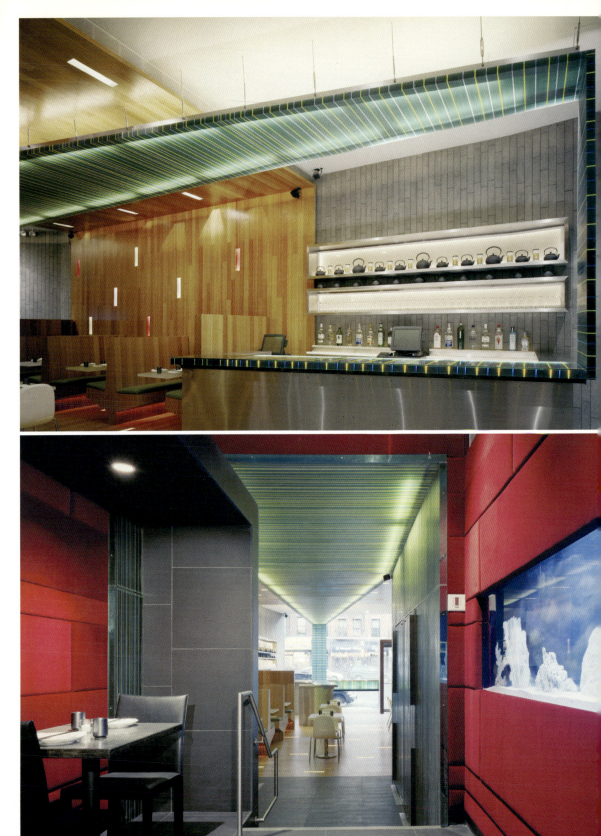

MASSIMILIANO FUKSAS/DORIANA MANDRELLI & MASSIMILIANO FUKSAS | ROME
ARMANI/THREE ON THE BUND
Shanghai, China | 2004

Armani/Three on the Bund is located in the lower floor of an historic building in Shanghai and boasts 1100 m² of floor space. Plastic is one of the materials used in the interior design. The flooring, perhaps the most outstanding feature of the space, is made from pale blue epoxy resin which has been given a shiny finish, thus transmitting to the customers the image of quality and luxury associated with the brand.

Armani/Three on the Bund befindet sich im Erdgeschoss eines historischen Gebäudes in Shanghai. Das Lokal ist 1.100 Quadratmeter groß. Kunststoff ist eines der Materialien, das bei der Innengestaltung benutzt wurde. Der Bodenbelag, vielleicht das auffallendste Element in diesem Raum, besteht aus blassblauem Expoxydharz mit einer glänzenden Oberfläche. Der Boden wirkt ebenso luxuriös und warm wie die Marke auf den Käufer wirken soll.

Armani/Three on the Bund está situado en la planta baja de un edificio histórico de Shangai y cuenta con 1.100 metros cuadrados de superficie. El plástico es uno de los materiales utilizados en su interiorismo. El pavimento, quizá el elemento más destacado del espacio, es de resina epoxídica de color azul pálido, a la que se le ha dado un acabado brillante que transmite al comprador la imagen de lujo y calidad asociada a la marca.

Armani/Three on the Bund est situé au rez-de-chaussée d'un monument historique de Shanghai et compte 1 100 mètres carrés de superficie. Le plastique est l'un des matériaux employés pour sa décoration intérieure. Le revêtement, peut être l'élément les plus en évidence de l'espace, est en résine époxy bleue pâle ayant reçu une finition brillante qui transmet à l'acheteur l'image de luxe et de qualité associée à la marque.

L'Armani/Three on the Bund di 1.100 metri quadrati si trova al piano terra di un edificio storico di Shanghai. La plastica è uno dei materiali usati per i suoi interni. Il pavimento, forse l'elemento di maggior rilievo dello spazio, è di resina epossidica blu chiaro, con una rifinitura brillante che trasmette al cliente l'immagine di lusso e qualità associato alla marca.

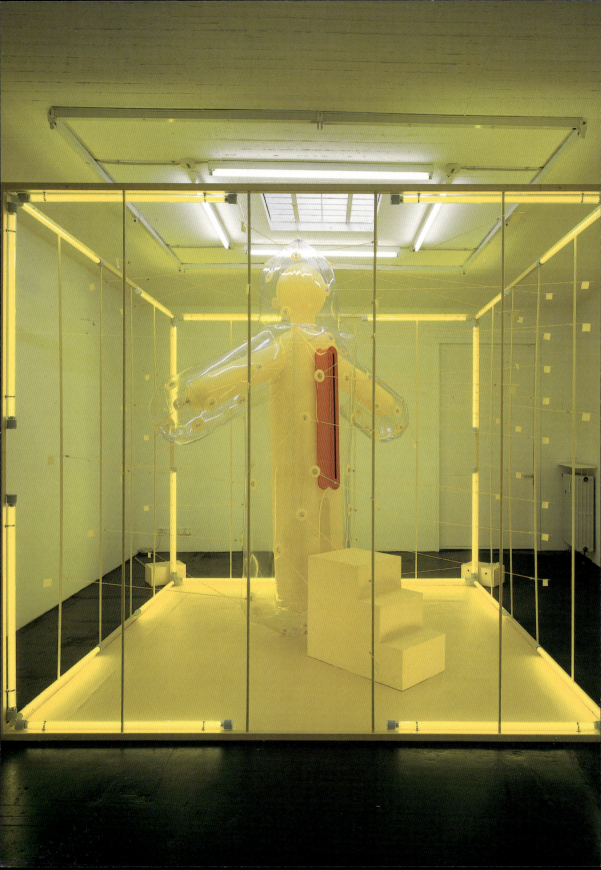

MATALI CRASSET | PARIS
CASADERME, POP UP SPACE, UPDATE 3 SPACES IN ONE
2002

Matali Crasset, the French designer belonging to the creative wave started by Phillipe Starck, has reinterpreted the concept of the traditional dwelling, as well as the spaces it holds (such as the bathroom), in many of its installations and projects. Plastic is the material which has allowed her to build prototypes and installations which could help overcome the problematic areas of interior design and contemporary architecture.

Matali Crasset, eine französische Designerin, die zu der kreativen Gruppe gehört, die von Philippe Starck begonnen wurde, hat das Konzept der traditionellen Wohnung in verschiedenen Installationen und Projekten neu interpretiert, ebenso wie die Räume, die dazu gehören, wie zum Beispiel das Badezimmer. Kunststoff ist das Material, aus dem die Prototypen und Installationen hergestellt wurden. Sie zeigen, dass dieses Material viele Möglichkeiten bietet, die man bisher in der zeitgenössischen Architektur und Innenarchitektur nicht zu nutzen wusste.

Matali Crasset –diseñadora francesa perteneciente a la estirpe creativa iniciada con Philippe Starck– ha reinterpretado el concepto de vivienda tradicional, así como el de los espacios que la componen (el cuarto de baño, por ejemplo), en varias de sus instalaciones y proyectos. El plástico es el material que le ha permitido construir prototipos e instalaciones que suponen una llamada de atención sobre las posibilidades desaprovechadas del diseño de interiores y la arquitectura contemporánea.

Matali Crasset, créatrice française appartenant à la ligne créative initiée avec Philippe Starck, a réinterprété le concept de maison traditionnelle ainsi que celui des espaces la composant (la salle de bains par exemple) dans plusieurs de ses installations et projets. Le plastique est le matériau qui lui a permis de construire prototypes et installations impliquant de susciter l'attention sur les possibilités gaspillées du design d'intérieur et de l'architecture contemporaine.

Matali Crasset –designer francese appartenente alla stirpe creativa iniziata da Philippe Starck– ha reinterpretato il concetto della casa tradizionale, come pure degli spazi che la compongono (il bagno, per esempio), in varie delle sue installazioni e progetti. La plastica è il materiale che le ha consentito di costruire prototipi ed installazioni capaci di attrarre l'attenzione sulle possibilità non sfruttate dal design degli interni e dall'architettura contemporanea.

CASADERME
una casa/pelle, elastica e traspirante

un mutante che assorbe contesto e oggetti quotidiani per costruire un intenso connettivo

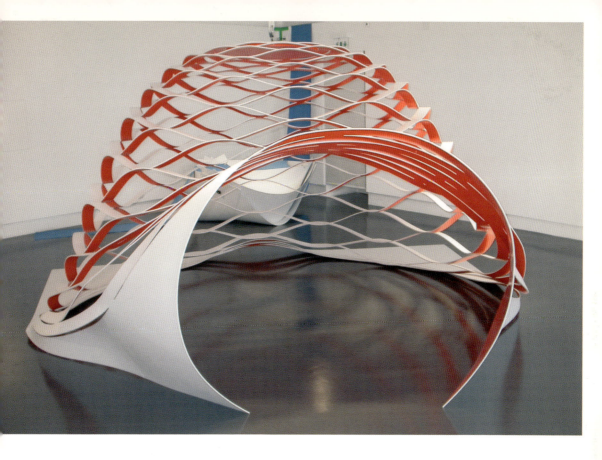

In 2001, the old office of the Australian architects Neil & Idle, now split into NFORM Architects and Idle Architecture Studio, won the Commercial Building Award of the State Architecture Awards, thanks, in part, to the impressive polycarbonate wall which covers its facade. In the interior, plastic is also one the materials most used, which gives the offices character and connects the interior and exterior, thus establishing a fluid dialogue between both zones.

Das ehemalige Studio der australischen Architekten Neil & Idle, das sich jetzt in NFORM Architects und Idle Architecture Studio gespalten hat, gewann 2001 den Preis Commercial Building Award der State Architecture Awards. Teilweise ist dieser Preis der auffallenden Wand aus Polykarbonat zu verdanken, die die Fassade verdeckt. Im Inneren der Büros ist Kunststoff ebenfalls eines der am meisten verwendeten Materialien, das dem Raum Persönlichkeit gibt und innen mit außen so verbindet, so dass ein Dialog zwischen beiden Bereichen entsteht.

La antigua oficina de los arquitectos australianos Neil & Idle, ahora divididos en NFORM Architects e Idle Architecture Studio, ganó en 2001 el Commercial Building Award de los State Architecture Awards gracias, en parte, a la espectacular pared de policarbonato que recubre su fachada. En el interior de las oficinas el plástico es también uno de los materiales más utilizados, el que les confiere personalidad y el que conecta interior y exterior estableciendo un diálogo fluido entre ambas zonas.

Les anciens bureaux des architectes australiens Neil & Idle, aujourd'hui NFORM Architects et Idle Architecture Studio, ont remporté en 2001 le Commercial Building Award des State Architecture Awards grâce, notamment, au mur spectaculaire en polycarbonate recouvrant leur façade. À l'intérieur des bureaux, le plastique est également l'une des matières de prédilection, celle leur offrant leur personnalité et connectant extérieur et intérieur en établissant un dialogue fluide entre les deux zones.

L'antico studio degli architetti australiani Neil & Idle, adesso divisi in NFORM Architects ed Idle Architecture Studio, ha vinto nel 2001 il Premio Commercial Building degli State Architecture Awards grazie, in parte, alla spettacolare parete in policarbonato che riveste la sua facciata. Dentro gli uffici la plastica è uno dei materiali più usati, che conferisce personalità e collega l'interno e l'esterno stabilendo un dialogo fluido tra le zone.

The Green Street Townhouses stand out due to the use of a material called modwood, a mix of plastic and wood. Likewise, some details in the interior spaces have plastic finishes or have been made with Perspex. The mixed materials allow the beneficial characteristics of plastic to be heightened and give the surface or covering in question a finish completely different from the traditional aesthetic of the material.

Die Green Street Townhouses zeichnen sich durch die Verwendung von Verkleidungen und Abdeckungen aus einem Material auf, das als „modwood" bezeichnet wird, ein Verbundstoff aus Kunststoff und Holz. Ebenso sind einige der Elemente in den Innenräume mit Kunststoff verkleidet oder aus Plexiglas konstruiert. Verbundmaterialien machen es möglich, die Vorteile des Kunststoffs zu nützen und gleichzeitig eine Verkleidung oder eine Fläche visuell so zu gestalten, dass sie ästhetisch nichts mehr mit dem gemein hat, was man im allgemeinen mit dieser Art von Materialien assoziiert.

Las Green Street Townhouses destacan por la utilización en revestimientos y cubiertas de un material llamado *modwood*, un compuesto de plástico y madera. Asimismo, algunos detalles en los espacios interiores cuentan con acabados plastificados o han sido fabricados con plexiglás. Los materiales compuestos permiten aprovechar las características ventajosas del plástico, dándole al revestimiento, o a la superficie de la que se trate, un acabado que visualmente no tiene nada que ver con la estética que asociamos tradicionalmente a este material.

Les Green Street Townhouses sont remarquables de par l'utilisation pour les revêtements et les couvertes d'une matière nommée modwood, un composé de plastique et de bois. De la sorte, certains détails des espaces intérieurs comptent des finitions plastifiées ou ont été fabriqués en perspex. Les matériaux composés permettent de tirer parti des caractéristiques avantageuses du plastique en offrant au revêtement, ou à la surface concernée, une finition totalement étrangère à l'esthétique que nous associons traditionnellement à ce matériau.

Le Green Street Townhouses spiccano per i rivestimenti e le coperture realizzate in un materiale chiamato *modwood*, un composto di plastica e legno. Inoltre, alcuni dettagli negli spazi interni presentano delle rifiniture plastificate, o sono stati fabbricati con del plexiglas. I materiali composti consentono di sfruttare le caratteristiche vantaggiose della plastica, dando al rivestimento, o alla superficie trattata, una finitura che visivamente non ha nulla da vedere con l'estetica che associamo tradizionalmente a questo materiale.

BIZARRE
Omaha, USA | 2005

Randy Brown had three objectives in this project: to experiment with new ways of maximizing the available space, to create a feeling of visual continuity between the elements of the shop and the interior
surfaces and to design a fluid space where artistic objects could be exhibited. The project includes various modules built with glass and acrylic materials, whose visual lightness creates an optical illusion
whereby the exhibited objects appear to be floating in mid air. The dynamic design of the shop was a
result of observing the folds in a piece of paper.

Randy Brown hatte sich bei dieser Planung drei Ziele gesetzt, mit neuen Methoden zu experimentieren,
um den zur Verfügung stehenden Raum optimal zu nützen, den Eindruck einer visuellen Kontinuität zwischen den Elementen des Geschäftes und den Flächen im Inneren zu schaffen und einen fließenden
Raum zu entwerfen, in dem Kunstwerke ausgestellt werden. Es wurden verschiedene Module aus Acryl
und Glas konstruiert, deren visuelle Leichtigkeit den Eindruck entstehen lässt, dass die ausgestellten
Objekte in der Luft schweben. Die Idee zu der dynamischen Gestaltung des Geschäftes entstand beim
Betrachten der Falten eines Blattes Papier.

Tres eran los objetivos de Randy Brown en este proyecto: experimentar con nuevas maneras de maxi-
mizar el espacio disponible, crear sensación de continuidad visual entre los elementos de la tienda y las
superficies interiores y diseñar un espacio fluido en el que exponer objetos artísticos. El proyecto cuenta con varios módulos construidos con materiales acrílicos y con vidrio, cuya ligereza visual crea la sensación de que los objetos expuestos están flotando en el aire. El dinámico diseño de la tienda surgió
tras observar los pliegues de una hoja de papel.

Randy Brown avait trois objectifs pour ce projet : expérimenter de nouvelles méthodes de maximiser
l'espace disponible, créer une sensation de continuité visuelle entre les éléments de la boutique et les
surfaces intérieures et concevoir un espace fluide où exposer des objets artistiques. Le projet compte
plusieurs modules construits avec des matériaux acryliques et du verre, dont la légèreté visuelle crée
l'illusion que les objets exposés flottent dans l'air. Le design dynamique de la boutique est né de l'observation des plis d'une feuille de papier.

Tre erano gli obiettivi di Randy Brown in questo progetto: sperimentare nuovi modi di massimizzare lo spazio disponibile, creare una sensazione di continuità visiva tra gli elementi del negozio e le superfici inter-
ne, e disegnare uno spazio fluido in cui esporre oggetti artistici. Il progetto conta con vari moduli costrui-
ti con materiali acrilici e vetro, questa leggerezza visiva dà l'idea che gli oggetti esposti fluttuino nell'aria.
Il design dinamico del negozio trae ispirazione dall'osservazione delle pieghe di un foglio di carta.

Randy Brown's project for this Omaha company gives all the importance to the juxtaposition of wooden and metal panels and the use of Plexiglas dividers. The result is a dynamic space of heterodox and irregular distribution, in which it is enjoyable to work and in the words of John Luce, the workers have doubled their productivity. The fact that all the joints and the beams are visible enhances this effect.

Dieses Projekt von Randy Brown für ein Unternehmen in Omaha basiert auf der Gegenüberstellung von Paneelen aus Holz und Metall zu Raumteilern aus Plexiglas. So entstand ein dynamischer, unregelmäßig aufgeteilter und heterodoxer Raum, in dem man gerne arbeitet und aufgrund dessen, nach eigenen Worten von John Luce, die Arbeiter ihre Produktivität verdoppelt haben. Da man sowohl die Fugen als auch die Balken der Struktur unverdeckt ließ, wird die beschriebene Wirkung noch verstärkt.

El proyecto de Randy Brown para esta empresa de Omaha concede todo el protagonismo a la yuxtaposición de paneles de madera y metal y al uso de divisores de plexiglás. El resultado es un espacio dinámico, de distribución irregular y heterodoxa, en el que resulta agradable trabajar y gracias al cual (en palabras del mismo John Luce) los trabajadores han doblado su productividad. El hecho de haber dejado a la vista tanto las junturas como las vigas de la estructura contribuye al efecto mencionado.

Le projet de Randy Brown pour cette entreprise d'Omaha braque tous les projecteurs sur la juxtaposition des panneaux de bois et de métal et l'usage de divisions en plexiglas. Il en résulte un espace dynamique à la distribution irrégulière et hétérodoxe où il est agréable de travailler et grâce auquel (pour citer John Luce lui-même), les travailleurs ont doublé leur productivité. Le fait d'avoir laissé apparents tant les raccords que les poutres de la structure contribue à l'effet mentionné.

Il progetto di Randy Brown per questa ditta d'Omaha concede tutto il protagonismo all'abbinamento di pannelli di legno e metallo, ed all'uso di divisori in plexiglas. Il risultato è uno spazio dinamico, dalla distribuzione irregolare ed eterodossa, dov'è gradevole lavorare e grazie al quale (secondo le parole stesse di John Luce) i dipendenti hanno raddoppiato la loro produttività. Il fatto di aver lasciato alla vista tanto le giunture quanto le travi della struttura, contribuisce al citato effetto.

Two thirty year olds decided to open their own clothes shop «in the style of New York's Soho» due to the lack of a similar outlet in Omaha, a typical town of the American Mid West. A minimalist space was thus designed with the roof in view and using acrylic materials which met all the desired requisites, one of which was the project's limited budget. The reticulated wall at the back of the shop acts as the core visual attraction of the space.

Zwei Frauen um die dreißig beschlossen, ihr eigenes Kleidergeschäft im „Stil des New Yorker Soho" zu eröffnen, weil sie der Ansicht waren, dass ein derartiges Angebot in Omaha, einer typischen Stadt im mittleren amerikanischen Westen, fehlte. Zu diesem Zweck wurde ein minimalistischer Raum mit unverkleideten Decken und Acrylmaterialien entworfen, der alle Voraussetzungen erfüllte, die man zu Anfang festlegte. Dazu gehörte auch, dass ein gewisses Budget nicht überschritten werden durfte. Die rasterförmige Wand hinten im Laden bildet einen visuellen Blickpunkt im Raum.

Dos treintañeras decidieron abrir su propia tienda de ropa «al estilo del Soho neoyorquino» decepcionadas frente a la falta de ofertas similares en Omaha, una ciudad típica del medio oeste americano. Con ese objeto se diseñó un espacio minimalista de cubiertas a la vista y materiales acrílicos que cumple todos los requisitos planteados en un principio, entre ellos el de que el proyecto se ajustara a un presupuesto limitado. La pared reticulada al fondo de la tienda actúa como referente visual del espacio.

Deux trentenaires ont décidé d'ouvrir leur propre boutique de mode « au style du Soho new-yorkais », déçues par le manque d'offres similaires à Omaha, une ville typique du Midwest américain. Pour elle, le design a imaginé un espace minimaliste de couvertes visibles et de matières acryliques respectant tous les impératifs originels, notamment le fait que le projet devait s'ajuster à un budget limité. La paroi réticulée au fond du magasin agit comme un foyer d'attention visuel de l'espace.

Due trentenni hanno deciso d'aprire un negozio d'abbigliamento «in stile Soho newyorchino» deluse dall'assenza di simili offerte ad Omaha, una tipica città del mid-west americano. Seguendo quest'idea è stato concepito uno spazio minimalista con coperture a vista e materiali acrilici che rispondono a tutti i requisiti decisi all'inizio, tra cui quello di far rientrare il progetto in un budget limitato. La parete reticolata del fondo del negozio agisce da referente visivo dello spazio.

The Melbourne Bureau of Meteorology's oval shaped meeting rooms have a semi transparent polypropylene covering which brings visual lightness to the space and allows the natural flow of light to flood the room. The result is a dynamic space of attractive curved shapes which creates a calm and tranquil ambience. Aesthetically speaking, the oval rooms are without doubt the focus of visual attention of the building, even from outside.

Die ovalen Versammlungssäle des Bureau of Meteorology in Melbourne sind mit halbtransparenten Polypropylen verkleidet, das den Raum visuell leicht wirken und reichlich Licht einströmen lässt. So entstand ein dynamischer Raum mit liebenswürdigen, gebogenen Formen, der sehr ruhig und einladend wirkt. Ohne Zweifel sind die ovalen Säle der visuelle Anziehungspunkt des Gebäudes, sogar von außen gesehen.

Las salas de reunión ovaladas del Bureau of Meteorology de Melbourne cuentan con un revestimiento de polipropileno semitransparente que confiere ligereza visual al espacio y permite que la luz procedente del exterior inunde la sala. El resultado es un espacio dinámico y de formas curvas amables que propicia una atmósfera de recogimiento y tranquilidad. Estéticamente, las salas ovaladas son sin duda alguna el foco de atención visual del edificio, incluso vistas desde el exterior.

Les salles de réunions ovales du Bureau of Meteorology de Melbourne comportent un revêtement en polypropylène semi transparent qui confère à l'espace sa légèreté visuelle et permet à la lumière provenant de l'extérieur d'inonder la salle. En résulte un espace dynamique aux formes courbes plaisantes qui suscite une atmosphère de recueil et de tranquillité. Esthétiquement, les salles ovales sont, indubitablement, le centre d'attention visuelle de l'édifice, même vues depuis l'extérieur.

Le sale riunioni ovali del Bureau of Meteorology di Melbourne presentano un rivestimento in polipropilene semitrasparente che conferisce leggerezza visiva allo spazio, permettendo alla luce esterna d'inondare la sala. Il risultato è uno spazio dinamico, dalle morbide forme curve che offre un'atmosfera di raccoglimento e tranquillità. Esteticamente, le sale ovali sono senza dubbio il fulcro dell'attenzione visiva dell'edificio, anche dall'esterno.

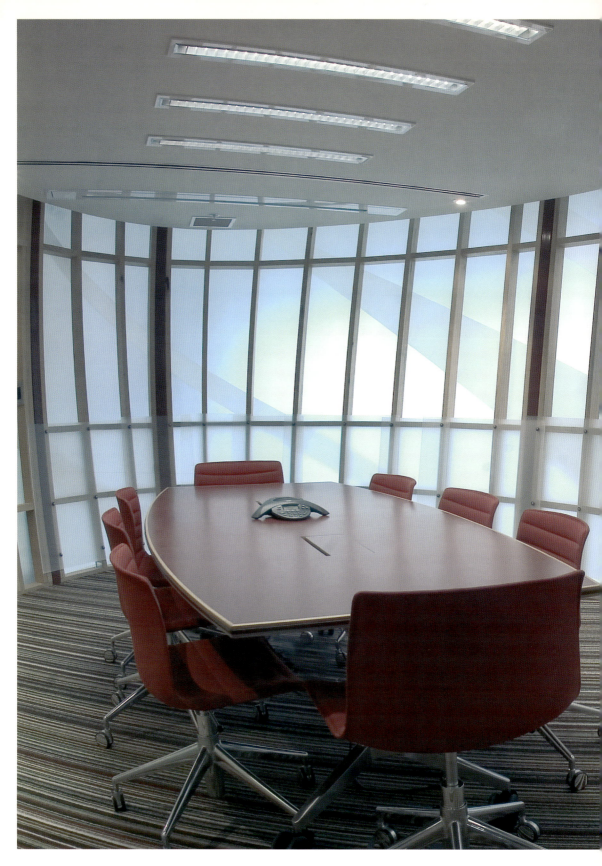

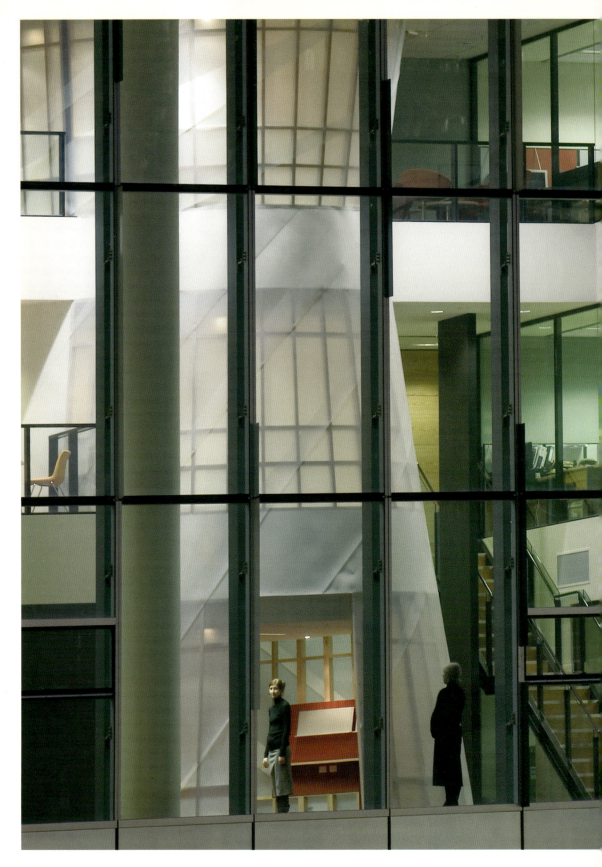

The partial reconstruction of this concert hall was handled by the architect Rudy Ricciotti on condition that the new space had to be acoustically up to date. The austere building is at the heart of a residential Baroque neighborhood of the old Potsdam and the most popular materials are copper and plastic.

Der Architekt Rudy Ricciotti wurde mit der teilweisen Rekonstruktion dieses Konzertsaales beauftragt. Ihm wurde die Aufgabe gestellt, dass der neue Raum den akustischen Anforderungen eines modernen Konzertsaales entsprechen musste. Das schlichte Gebäude befindet sich im Herzen eines barocken Wohnviertels im alten Potsdam. Zu den hauptsächlich für die Struktur verwendeten Materialien gehören Kupfer und Kunststoff.

La reconstrucción parcial de esta sala de conciertos le fue encargada al arquitecto Rudy Ricciotti con la premisa de que el nuevo espacio debía adecuarse a las necesidades acústicas de las salas de conciertos contemporáneas. El edificio se levanta, austero, en el corazón de un barroco barrio residencial del viejo Potsdam y cuenta con el cobre y el plástico como algunos de los materiales más utilizados en su estructura.

La reconstruction partielle de cette salle de concert fut confiée à l'architecte Rudy Ricciotti avec une prémisse : le nouvel espace devait s'adapter aux impératifs acoustiques des salles de concert contemporaines. L'édifice s'élève, austère, au cœur d'un quartier résidentiel baroque du vieux Potsdam et compte le cuivre et le plastique parmi les matériaux privilégiés pour sa structure.

La ricostruzione parziale di questa sala concerti è stata commissionata all'architetto Rudy Ricciotti, con la premessa che il nuovo spazio doveva adeguarsi alle necessità acustiche delle sale concerti contemporanee. L'edificio si erge austero nel cuore di un quartiere residenziale barocco della vecchia Potsdam, ed ha nel rame e la plastica alcuni dei materiali più usati nella sua struttura.

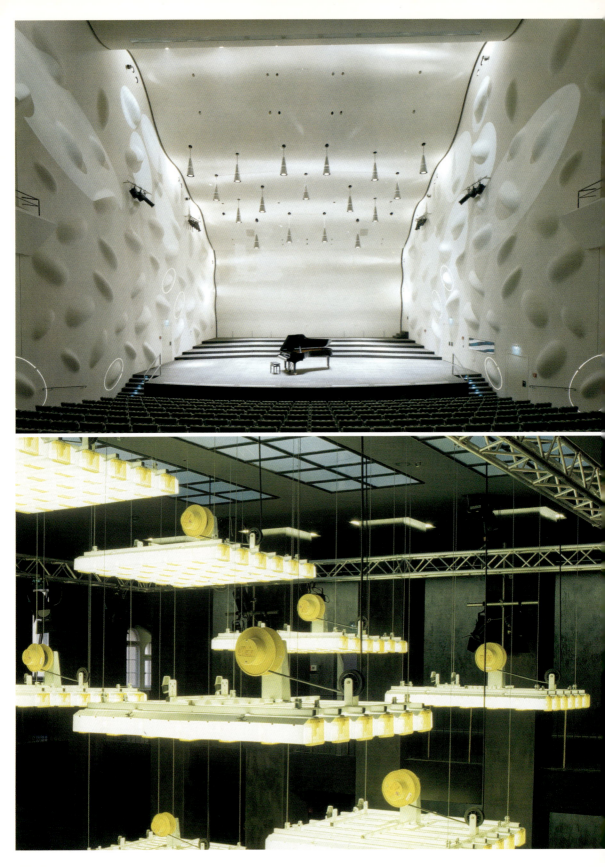

The renovation of the Greenberg Van Doren gallery respected the existing structure of approximately 1100 m², in order to create a completely new space divided into three clearly different zones: the gallery itself, the offices and the storage area. In the offices' zone which also houses a library and a meeting area, a plastic ceiling with a shiny, reflecting finish was used which serves as a mirror and visually doubles the height of the room.

Bei der Renovierung der Galerie Greenberg Van Doren wurde die bereits existierende, ungefähr 1.100 Quadratmeter große Struktur respektiert, um einen komplett neuen Raum zu schaffen, der sich in drei klar voneinander getrennte Bereiche unterteilt, die Galerie selbst, die Büro und die Lagerräume. Im Bürobereich, in dem sich auch eine Bibliothek und ein Versammlungssaal befinden, wurde eine Decke aus glänzendem Kunststoff geschaffen, die wie ein Spiegel reflektiert und so die Höhe des Raums visuell verdoppelt.

La reforma de la galería Greenberg Van Doren respetó la estructura preexistente, de aproximadamente 1.100 metros cuadrados de planta, para crear un espacio completamente nuevo, dividido en tres zonas claramente diferenciadas: la galería en sí, las oficinas y la zona de almacenamiento. En el área de oficinas, que también alberga una biblioteca y la sala de reuniones, se recurrió a un techo plástico de acabado brillante y reflectante que actúa como un espejo, doblando visualmente la altura de la estancia.

La réforme de la galerie Greenberg Van Doren a respecté la structure préexistante, d'une surface approchant les 1 100 mètres carrés, pour créer un espace complètement nouveau divisé en trois zones clairement différenciées : la galerie elle-même, les bureaux et la zone d'entreposage. Dans la partie bureaux, qui accueille également une bibliothèque et la zone de réunion, a été retenu un plafond de plastique à la finition brillante et réfléchissante qui agit comme un miroir, doublant visuellement la hauteur du lieu.

La ristrutturazione della galleria Greenberg Van Doren, ha rispettato la struttura preesistente, di circa 1.100 metri quadrati di pianta, per creare uno spazio completamente nuovo diviso in tre zone ben differenti: la galleria da per sé, gli uffici e la zona del magazzino. Nell'area uffici, in cui si trova anche una biblioteca e la sala riunione, si è ricorsi ad un tetto di plastica con rifinitura brillante e riflettente che funge da specchio capace di raddoppiare visivamente l'altezza della sala.

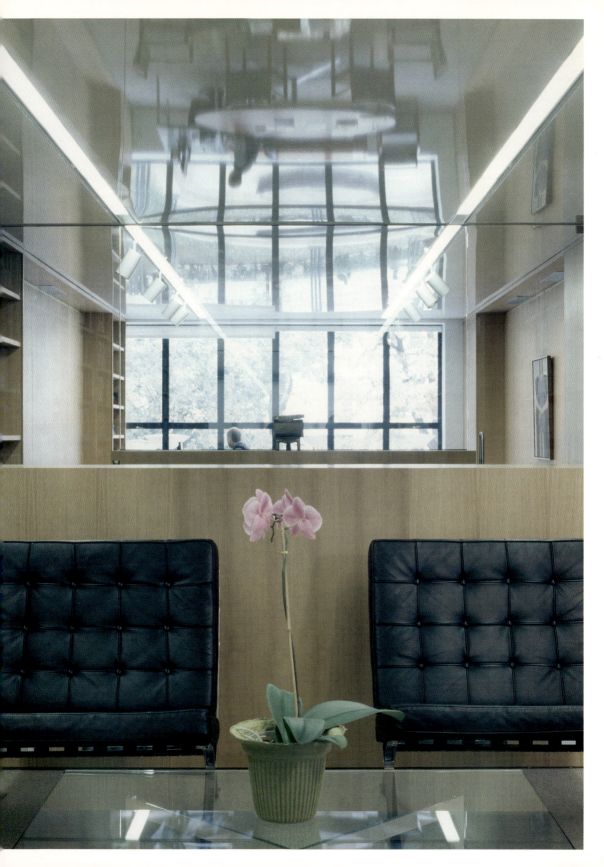

Plastic and more specifically resin is the material which gives a retro futuristic air to this Miami apartment. Both the desk and the bed have been manufactured using fiber glass and resin and the floor also is made from resin. The shiny finish of the plastic features and their rounded shapes apparent throughout the apartment are another point of interest.

Kunststoff, genauer gesagt, Kunststoffharz ist das Material, das dieser Wohnung in Miami ihren ganz besonderen, retrofuturistischen Charakter verleiht. Sowohl der Schreibtisch als auch das Bett im Schlafzimmer wurden aus Glasfaser und Kunststoffharz konstruiert. Auch für den Bodenbelag verwendete man Kunststoffharz. Die glänzenden Oberflächen der synthetischen Elemente und ihre runden Formen findet man überall in der Wohnung in kleinen Details, was zu interessanten Effekten führt.

El plástico, y más concretamente la resina, es el material que confiere una acusada personalidad retrofuturista a este apartamento de Miami. Tanto el escritorio como la cama del dormitorio han sido fabricados en fibra de vidrio y resina. La resina es también el material utilizado como pavimento. El acabado brillante de los elementos sintéticos y sus formas redondeadas, presentes en multitud de detalles del apartamento, son otro de sus atractivos.

Le plastique, et plus concrètement la résine, est la matière qui confère une forte personnalité rétrofuturiste à cet appartement de Miami. Le bureau tout comme le lit de la chambre à coucher ont été fabriqués en fibre de verre et en résine. La résine a également été retenue pour revêtir les sols. La finition brillante des éléments plastiques et leurs formes arrondies, présentes dans une foule de détails de l'appartement, constituent un autre de ses charmes.

La plastica, e più in concreto la resina, è la materia che conferisce una forte personalità retrofuturista a quest'appartamento di Miami. Il tavolo ed il letto della stanza sono stati realizzati in fibra di vetro e resina, materiale prescelto anche per il pavimento. La finitura brillante degli elementi sintetici e le sue forme arrotondate, presenti in tanti dettagli dell'appartamento, sono altri elementi interessanti.

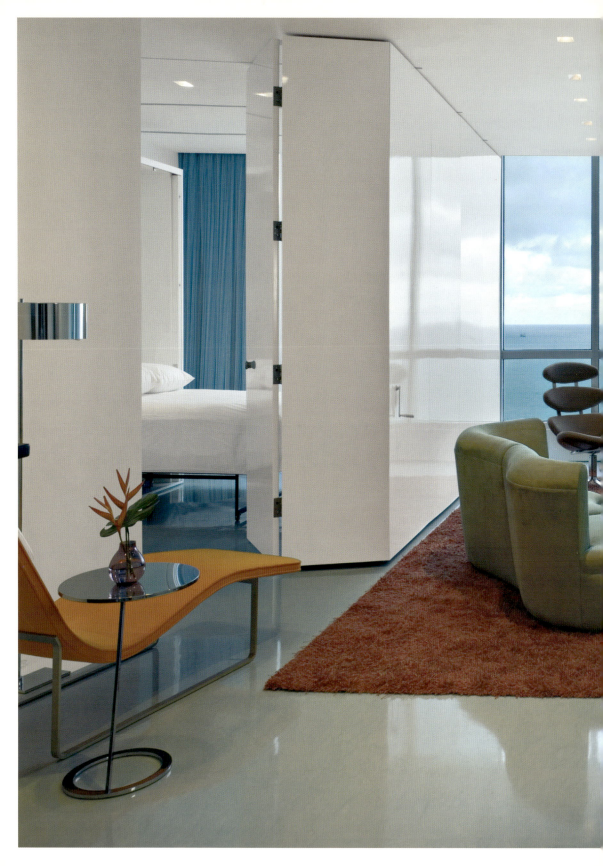

Marblo, a polymer material which is manufactured in standard sized sheets but which can be adapted to the needs of the architect or designer, is the material with which the furniture and fittings have been made from in this Australian residence. Marblo can be made in any color and with any level of transparency which is why it has been used here to exaggerate the effect of the spatial depth of the dwelling. The illumination of the features made in marblo, by way of fitted zenithal spot lights and interior luminaries reinforce this effect of depth.

Marblo, ein Polymer, das in Form von Lamellen in einem Standardformat vertrieben wird, die jedoch geschnitten werden können, um sie für gestalterische Zwecke zu verwenden, ist das Material, aus dem die Möbel in diesem Haus in Australien konstruiert wurden. Marblo kann man in jeder Farbe und verschiedenen Graden von Transparenzen herstellen. Deshalb wählte man dieses Material für diesen Umbau, bei dem man den Eindruck einer besonders großen räumlichen Tiefe erwecken wollte. Die Beleuchtung der Elemente aus Marblo durch eingebaute Deckenlampen und indirekte Beleuchtung verstärkt diesen Eindruck der Tiefe noch.

El marblo, un material polimérico que se comercializa en láminas de tamaños estándar pero que puede ser recortado para ajustarse a las necesidades del arquitecto o del diseñador, es el material con el que se ha realizado el mobiliario de esta residencia australiana. El marblo puede ser fabricado en cualquier color y en cualquier grado de transparencia que se desee, de ahí que haya sido el material escogido en una reforma en la que se pretendía crear un exagerado efecto de profundidad espacial. La iluminación de los elementos fabricados en marblo, mediante focos cenitales empotrados o luminarias interiores, reafirma ese efecto de profundidad.

Le marblo, un matériau polymère qui se fabrique en feuilles de taille standard mais peut être découpé pour s'ajuster aux besoins de l'architecte ou du créateur, est la matière ayant présidé à la fabrication du mobilier de cette résidence australienne. Le marblo peut être fabriqué dans toutes les couleurs et selon tous les niveaux de transparence souhaités. Pour ces raisons, il a été retenu dans le cadre d'une réforme qui prétendait créer un effet exagéré de profondeur spatiale. L'illumination des éléments fabriqués en marblo, avec des spots zénithaux encastrés ou des luminaires intérieurs, réaffirme cet effet de profondeur.

Il marblo, un materiale polimerico venduto in lamine di dimensioni standard, ma che può essere tagliato secondo le necessità dell'architetto o del designer, è il materiale scelto per realizzare i mobili di questa casa australiana. Il marblo può essere prodotto in qualsiasi colore e grado di trasparenza necessario, e per questo è stato prescelto come materiale in una ristrutturazione che voleva creare un esagerato effetto di profondità spaziale. L'illuminazione degli elementi realizzati in marblo, mediante spot zenitali incassati o lumi interni, riaffermano l'effetto di profondità.

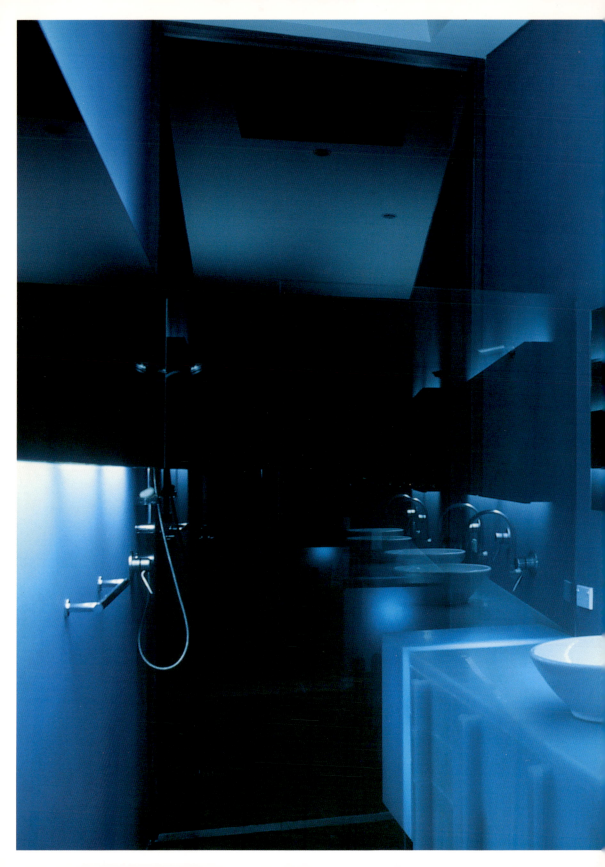

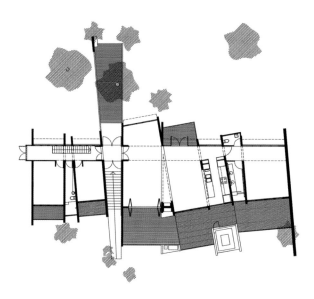

Plastic is a ductile, flexible and above all a material which is adaptable to practically any decorative style thanks to its availability in any color or level of transparency or hardness. In the case of the Skefjar project, plastic is practically an ever-present material: it can be seen as PEH, in tables, lamps, translucent panes (e.g. the kitchen walls) and as rubber and latex in the luminaries, designed by Signy Kólbeinsdóttir.

Kunststoff ist ein dehnbares, elastisches und vor allem an jeden Dekorationsstil anpassbares Material, da man es in verschiedenen Farben, Härten und Transparenzen finden kann. In diesem Projekt von Skefjar ist Kunststoff das Material, das praktisch überall zu finden ist; in Form von PEH (Polyethylen) an den Tischen, Lampen und lichtdurchlässigen Paneelen (z. B. die Küchenwand), und in Form von Gummi und Latex an den Lampen, die von Signy Kólbeinsdóttir entworfen wurden.

El plástico es un material dúctil, flexible y, sobre todo, adaptable a prácticamente cualquier estilo decorativo, gracias a encontrarse disponible en diferentes colores y grados de transparencia y de dureza. En el caso del proyecto Skefjar, el plástico es un material prácticamente omnipresente: lo podemos encontrar en forma de PEH (polietileno) en mesas, lámparas y paneles translúcidos (la pared de la cocina, por ejemplo) y en forma de goma y látex en las luminarias, diseñadas por Signy Kólbeinsdóttir.

Le plastique est une matière ductile, flexible et, surtout, adaptable à pratiquement tout style décoratif car il est disponible en couleurs et niveaux de transparence et dureté différents. Dans le cas du projet Skefjar, le plastique est un matériau pratiquement omniprésent : nous le retrouvons sous la forme de PEH (polyéthylène) dans les tables, lampes et panneaux translucides (le mur de la cuisine par exemple) et sous forme de caoutchouc et de latex dans les luminaires, créés par Signy Kólbeinsdóttir.

La plastica è una materia duttile, flessibile e, soprattutto, adattabile a quasi tutti gli stili decorativi, grazie al fatto d'essere disponibile in vari colori, gradi di trasparenza, e di durezza. Nel caso del progetto di Skefjar, la plastica è un materiale praticamente onnipresente: si ritrova sotto forma di PEH (polietilene) in tavoli, lampade e pannelli translucidi (la parete della cucina, per esempio), sotto forma di gomma, e latex per i lumi, disegnati da Signy Kólbeinsdóttir.

The Ohno bus stop is found in Oita, a Japanese town situated between various mountains and with a population of about 5000. The contrast between the visual density and heaviness of the cement and the lightness of plastic gives a «rhythm» required by the architect. The two structures of the bus stop have plastic walls with different levels of transparency – the toilet one is opaque, while the waiting room one is completely translucent in order to maximize light flow.

Der Busbahnhof Ohno befindet sich in Oita, einer japanischen Stadt in den Bergen mit ungefähr 5.000 Einwohnern. Der Gegensatz zwischen der Schwere und visuellen Dichte des Zements und der Leichtigkeit des Kunststoffs schafft den „Rhythmus", den der Architekt diesem Bau geben wollte. Die beiden Module des Busbahnhofs haben Wände aus Kunststoff mit unterschiedlicher Transparenz; die der Toiletten sind lichtundurchlässig, während die des Wartesaals vollkommen lichtdurchlässig sind, damit soviel Licht wie möglich in den Raum dringt.

La parada de autobús Ohno se encuentra en Oita, una localidad japonesa encajada entre montañas y con una población de aproximadamente 5.000 habitantes. El contraste entre la pesadez y densidad visual del cemento y la ligereza del plástico proporcionan el «ritmo» que el arquitecto deseaba imprimir al proyecto. Los dos módulos de la parada cuentan con paredes de plástico con un grado de transparencia distinto: el del lavabo es opaco, mientras que el de la sala de espera es completamente translúcido, para dejar pasar la mayor cantidad de luz posible.

L'arrêt d'autobus Ohno se trouve à Oita, une ville japonaise encaissée entre diverses montagnes et comptant environ 5 000 habitants. Le contraste entre la pesanteur et la densité visuelle du ciment et la légèreté du plastique fournit le « rythme » que l'architecte souhaitait imprimer au projet. Les deux modules de l'arrêt comptent des murs en plastique présentant un niveaux de transparence différencié : celui des toilettes est opaque alors que pour la salle d'attente il est complètement translucide, afin de laisser passer la plus grande quantité de lumière possible.

La fermata dell'autobus Ohna si trova ad Oita, una località giapponese incastrata tra le montagne, con una popolazione di circa 5.000 abitanti. Il contrasto tra la pesantezza e la densità visiva del cemento e la leggerezza della plastica, danno il «ritmo» che l'architetto desiderava imprimere al progetto. I due moduli della fermata presentano pareti di plastica con un diverso grado di trasparenza: quello del bagno è opaco, mentre quello della sala d'attesa è completamente translucido per lasciar passare quanta più luce possibile.

The extension of the offices and the warehouse of a company in Turin specializing in the manufacture of fiber optic applications and the use of advanced technologies in the field of artificial illumination was carried out by building a new 400 m² structure above the existing building. The chosen material for the facade is PMMA. Visually, plastic is radically different from the brick walls of the lower structure and gives the project a strong character.

Eine Erweiterung der Büros und des Lagers eines Unternehmens in Turin, das auf die Herstellung von Glasfaser und fortschrittliche Technologien im Bereich der künstlichen Beleuchtung spezialisiert ist, wurde durch den Bau eines neuen, 400 Quadratmeter großen Anbaus verwirklicht, der sich über dem bereits existierenden Gebäude befindet. Als Fassadenmaterial wählte man PMMA (Plexiglas). Visuell unterscheidet sich dieser Kunststoff radikal von den Ziegelwänden des unteren Teils, was dem Gebäude eine neue und sehr starke Persönlichkeit gibt.

La ampliación de las oficinas y el almacén de una empresa de Turín –especializada en la fabricación de aplicaciones de fibra óptica y el uso de tecnologías avanzadas en el terreno de la iluminación artificial– se llevó a cabo construyendo un nuevo volumen de 400 metros cuadrados de planta sobre el ya existente. El material escogido para la fachada fue PMMA (plexiglás). Visualmente, el plástico se diferencia radicalmente de las paredes de ladrillo del volumen inferior y confiere al proyecto una fuerte personalidad.

L'extension des bureaux et du magasin d'une entreprise de Turin spécialisée dans la fabrication d'applications de fibre optique et l'usage de technologies avancées dans le domaine de l'illumination artificielle a été menée à bien en construisant un nouveau volume de 400 mètres carrés de superficie, sur le volume existant. Le PMMA est le matériau retenu pour la façade. Visuellement, le plastique se différencie radicalement des parois de briques du volume inférieur et confère au projet une forte personnalité.

L'ampliamento degli uffici e del magazzino di una ditta di Torino –specializzata nella fabbricazione d'applicazioni di fibra ottica e l'uso di tecnologie avanzate nel campo dell'illuminazione artificiale– è stato realizzato costruendo un nuovo volume di 400 metri quadrati di pianta sopra quello esistente. Il materiale prescelto per la facciata è stato il PMMA (plexiglas). Visivamente, la plastica si differenzia radicalmente dalle pareti in mattoni del volume inferiore, dando al progetto una forte personalità.

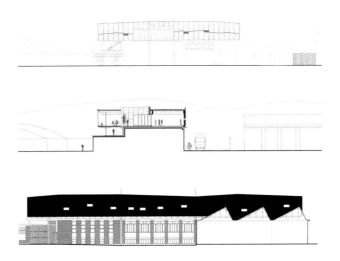

The interior architecture of the Arola restaurant, framed within a space created by the architects Jean Nouvel and the B-720 team and Albert Medem, is defined by the large variety of shapes, materials and textures present. The tables, made from a material called hi-macs, chosen for its durability, transparency and quality, act as distributors, separating the bar zone from the dining zone. The color white establishes an attractive architectural fluid yet tense dialogue with the roof of the auditorium designed by Nouvel.

Die Innengestaltung des Restaurants Arola, das sich in einem Gebäude des Architekten Jean Nouvel befindet, wurde von dem Team B-720 und Alberto Medem durchgeführt. Die Räumlichkeiten sind durch die Vielfalt der Formen, Materialien und Texturen charakterisiert. Die Tische bestehen aus einem Material, das als „hi-macs" bezeichnet wird, und das man aufgrund seiner Haltbarkeit, Transparenz und Qualität wählte. Sie dienen als Raumteiler und trennen den Bereich der Bar von den Bereich der Tische ab. Durch die Wahl der Farbe Weiß entstand ein auffallender architektonischer Dialog, fließend aber mit einer gewissen Spannung, mit dem Dach des Auditoriums, das von Nouvel entworfen wurde.

La arquitectura interior del restaurante Arola, enmarcado en un espacio concebido por los arquitectos Jean Nouvel, el equipo B-720 y Alberto Medem, se caracteriza por la gran variedad de formas, materiales y texturas presentes en ella. Las mesas, fabricadas en un material llamado *hi-macs*, escogido por su durabilidad, transparencia y calidad, actúan como distribuidoras separando la zona de la barra del área del comedor. El color escogido, el blanco, establece un llamativo diálogo arquitectónico, fluido pero tenso, con la cubierta del auditorio diseñado por Nouvel.

L'architecture intérieure du restaurant Arola, encadré dans un espace conçu par les architectes Jean Nouvel, l'équipe B-720 et Alberto Medem, se caractérise par la grande variété de formes, matériaux et textures en présence. Les tables, fabriquées en un matériau nommé hi-macs, retenu pour sa durabilité, sa transparence et sa qualité, agissent comme des distributeurs, séparant la zone du comptoir de la partie restauration. La couleur choisie −le blanc− établit un dialogue architectural saisissant, fluide mais tendu, avec la couverte de l'auditorium, création de Nouvel.

L'architettura interna del ristorante Arola, inserito in uno spazio concepito dagli architetti Jean Nouvel, il tema B-720 e Alberto Medem, si caratterizza per la gran varietà di forme, materiali e consistenze presenti. I tavoli, realizzati in un materiale chiamato *hi-macs* scelto per la sua tenuta nel tempo, trasparenza e qualità, agiscono come distributori separando la zona del bancone dall'area della sala da pranzo. Il colore prescelto, il bianco, instaura un peculiare dialogo architettonico, fluido ma teso, con la copertura dell'auditorio disegnato da Nouvel.

Fiber glass is normally used to strengthen and give greater mechanical resistance to the polyester resins. In this case it has been used for the exterior of this residence in amongst a woodland area of 6000 m². Its transparency filters the natural light flow into the house as well as giving it a visual lightness.

Glasfaser wird oft zum Verstärken von Polyesterharzen verwendet, die so eine größere mechanische Widerstandskraft erhalten. In diesem Fall wurde das Material für die äußeren Schilder an diesem Haus verwendet, das sich auf einem 6.000 Quadratmeter großen, bewaldeten Gelände befindet. Aufgrund seiner Transparenz wird die Intensität des Lichtes, das durch die Fenster fällt, abgeschwächt. Dennoch wird genügend Licht durchgelassen. Gleichzeitig lässt dieses leichte Material das Haus visuell schwerelos wirken.

La fibra de vidrio suele utilizarse para reforzar y proporcionar mayor resistencia mecánica a las resinas de poliéster. En este caso, ha sido el material utilizado para las viseras exteriores de esta residencia anclada en un terreno boscoso de 6.000 metros cuadrados. Su transparencia matiza la intensidad de la luz que entra por las ventanas, pero no impide su paso por completo. Al mismo tiempo, su ligereza confiere liviandad visual a la vivienda.

La fibre de verre est traditionnellement utilisée pour renforcer et offrir une plus grande résistance aux résines polyester. En l'occurrence, c'était le matériau utilisé pour les visières extérieures de cette résidence ancrée dans un terrain boisé de 6 000 mètres carrés. Sa transparence nuance la quantité de lumière qui entre par les fenêtres mais sans la bloquer complètement. Parallèlement, sa légèreté confère une certaine grâce visuelle à la demeure.

La fibra di vetro si usa in genere per rinforzare e dare maggiore resistenza meccanica alle resine di poliestere. In questo caso, è stato il materiale usato per le marchesine esterne di questa casa situata in un terreno boscoso di 6.000 metri quadrati. La loro trasparenza sfuma l'intensità della luce che entra dalle finestre, senza impedirne completamente l'ingresso. Al contempo, la loro leggerezza, alleggerisce visivamente la casa.

123 DV
St. Jobsweg 30 A, 3024 EJ Rotterdam, The Netherlands
P +31 (0)10 478 2064
F +31 (0)10 425 4764
info@123dv.nl
www.123dv.nl
Loft St. Jobsweg
Photos: © 123 DV

24h Architecture
Van Nelleweg 1206, Tabak 2.06, 3044 BC Rotterdam,
The Netherlands
P +31 (0)10 750 3150
F +31 (0)10 750 3160
info@24h.eu
www.24h.eu
Ichthus Business Centre
Photos: © Christian Richters

Alden Maddry
928 Lorimer Street 3, Brooklyn, New York, NY 11222, USA
P + 1 718 383 1947
F + 1 718 360 0487
am@aldenmaddry.com
www.aldenmaddry.com
Phillipps Skaife Residence
Photos: © Seong Kwon

B A R
Pelgrimstraat 5-B, NL 3029 BH Rotterdam, The Netherlands
P +31 (0)10 477 3863
F +31 (0)10 476 6615
info@bararchitects.com
www.bararchitects.com
Junkyhotel
Photos: © Rob't Hart
Mobilebox
Photos: © Rob't Hart

Behnisch Architekten
Rotebühlstrasse 163A, 70197 Stuttgart, Germany
P +49 711 607 720
F +49 711 607 7299
buero@behnisch.com
www.behnisch.com
Genzyme Center
Photos: © Anton Grassl

Bohlin Cywinski Jackson
1932 First Avenue, Suite 916, Seattle, WA 98101, USA
P + 1 206 256 0862
F + 1 206 256 0864
www.bcj.com
Gosline House
Photos: © Benjamin Benschneider

Brunete Fraccaroli
Rua Batataes, 460 Jd. Paulista, 01423-010 São Paulo, Brazil
P +55 11 3885 8309
F +55 11 3885 8309
brunete@osite.com.br
www.brunetefraccaroli.com.br
Singer's Loft
Photos: © Tuca Reinés

Buratti-Battiston Architects
Via Cellini 5, 20020 Busto Garolfo, Milan, Italy
P +39 033 156 9575
F +39 033 156 9063
studio@burattibattiston.it
www.burattibattiston.it
A.Shop, Intermot Fair
Photos: © Marino Ramazzotti

Concrete Architectural Associates
Rozengracht 133 III, 1016 LV Amsterdam, The Netherlands
P +31 (0)20 520 0200
F +31 (0)20 520 0201
info@concreteamsterdam.nl
www.concreteamsterdam.nl
The Mansion
Photos: © Jeroen Musch

Crepain Binst Architecture nv
Vlaanderenstraat 6, B 2000 Antwerp, Belgium
P +32 (0)3 213 6161
F +32 (0)3 213 6162
mail@crepainbinst.be
www.crepainbinst.be
Duval Guillaume
Photos: © Ludo Noël
Feyen Residence
Photos: © Ludo Noël

Curiosity
2-13-16 Tomigaya, Shibuya-ku, Tokyo 151-0063, Japan
P +81 3 5452 0095
F +81 3 5454 9691
info@curiosity.jp
www.curiosity.jp
Patisserie C-3
Photos: © Daici Ano

Daniele Claudio Taddei
Feldeggstrasse 54, 8008 Zürich, Switzerland
P +41 794 094 850
F +41 438 185 958
taddei@milnor.net
www.taddei-architect.com
Loft in Puls 5
Photos: © Bruno Helbling Fotografie

Desai-Chia Architecture
54 West 21st Street #703, New York, NY 10010, USA
P + 1 212 366 9630
F + 1 212 366 9278
info@desaichia.com
www.desaichia.com
Flower District Loft
Photos: © Joshua McHugh, Paul Warchol

Despang Architekten
Am Graswege 5, 30169 Hanover, Germany
P +49 511 882 840
F +49 511 887 985
Despang@BauNetz.de
www.despangarchitekten.de
238 Architecture
Hall West, PO Box 880107, Lincoln, NF 68588-0107, USA
P + 1 402 472 9956
F + 1 402 472 3806
mdespang@unlnotes.unl.edu
archweb.unl.edu
Kreipe's Coffeeshop
Photos: © Olaf Baumann, Joachim Giesel

Elliott & Associates Architects
35 Harrison Avenue, Oklahoma City, OK 73104, USA
P + 1 405 232 9554
F + 1 405 232 9997
design@e-a-a.com
www.e-a-a.com
ImageNet Carrollton
Photos: © Robert Shimer
ImageNet Oklahoma
Photos: © Robert Shimer

Giovannitti Inc.
18 Gibson Place, Yonkers, NY 10705, USA
P + 1 914 963 1744
F + 1 914 963 1190
dgiovannitti@optonline.net
Norman Jaffe. Romantic Modernist
Photos: © Andres Jost

Gracia Studio
4492 Camino de la Plaza, suite 1671,
San Diego, CA 92173, USA
P + 1 619 819 8323
F + 1 619 955 6877
jorge@graciastudio.com
www.graciastudio.com
Casa Ga
Photos: © Pablo Mason, Eduardo de Regules

Graser Architekten AG
Neugasse 6, 8005 Zürich, Switzerland
P +41 433 669 900
F +41 433 669 901
architekten@graser.ch
www.graser.ch
Via Mat Artcare
Photos: © Tobias Madörin

Hawkins-Brown
60 Bastwick Street, EC1V 3TN London, UK
P +44 020 7336 8030
F +44 020 7336 8851
mail@hawkinsbrown.co.uk
www.hawkinsbrown.co.uk
OQO
Photos: © Simon Phipps
The Culture House
Photos: © Keith Collie

Hertl Architekten
Zwischenbrücken 4, 4400 Steyr, Austria
P +43 7252 46944
F +43 7252 47363
steyr@hertl-architekten.com
www.hertl-architekten.com
Sauna / Greenhouse
Photos: © Paul Ott
Warehouse Hartlauer
Photos: © Paul Ott

Hugo Dworzak
Steinebach 3, 6850 Dornbirn, Austria
P +43 5572 34228
F +43 5572 55583
office@hugodworzak.at
www.austria-architects.com / hugo.dworzak
Terminal V
Photos: © Craig Kuhner

Infix Design Inc.
3F LAID Bld. 1-9-9 Nishihonmachi, Nishi-ku,
Osaka 550-0005, Japan
P +81 6 6110 1128
F +81 6 6534 0577
info@infix-sh.com
www.infix-design.com
GB Gafas Umeda
Photos: © Nacasa & Partners Inc.

Ivan Kroupa Architects
Osadni 41/46, 17000 Prague 6-Holesovice, Czech Republic
P +420 244 460 103
ivankroupa@ivankroupa.cz
www.ivankroupa.cz
BB Centre Reception
Photos: © Martin Rezabek

John Friedman-Alice Kimm Architects, Inc.
701 East 3rd Street, Suite 300, Los Angeles, CA 90013, USA
P + 1 213 253 4740
F + 1 213 253 4760
info@jfak.net
www.jfak.net
Club Sugar
Photos: © Benny Chan
L.A. Design Center Phase 1
Photos: © Benny Chan
The Brig
Photos: © Benny Chan

Jordan Mozer & Associates, Ltd.
320 West Ohio Street, 7th Floor, Chicago, IL 60610, USA
P + 1 312 543 3536
F + 1 312 397 1233
jordan@mozer.com
www.mozer.com
Canter's Deli
Photos: © Doug Snower
Karstadt
Photos: © Doug Snower
Nectar
Photos: © Doug Snower

Jordi Yaya Tur-Coloco Design
Av. Ragull 34, izquierda bajos, 08190 Sant Cugat,
Barcelona, Spain
P +34 619 255 122
F +34 936 754 373
yayatur@colocodesign.com
www.colocodesign.com
Clear
Photos: © Alejandro Bachrach

Kengo Kuma & Associates
2-24-8 BY CUBE 2-4F, Minamiaoyama Minato-ku,
Tokyo 107-0062, Japan
P +81 03 3401 7721
F +81 03 3401 7778
kuma@ba2.so-net.ne.jp
www.kkaa.co.jp
NTT Aoyama Renovation
Photos: © Daici Ano

Lewis-Tsurumaki-Lewis Architects
147 Essex Street, New York, NY 10002, USA
P + 1 212 505 5955
F + 1 212 505 1648
office@ltlwork.net
www.ltlarchitects.com
Xing Restaurant
Photos: © Michael Moran

Massimiliano Fuksas
Piazza del Monte di Pietà 30, 00186 Rome, Italy
P +39 066 880 7871
F +39 066 880 7872
office@fuksas.it
www.fuksas.it
Armani/Three on the Bund
Photos: © Giacomo Giannini

Matali Crasset
26 rue du Buisson Saint Louis, F-75010 Paris, France
P +33 1 42 40 99 89
F +33 1 42 40 99 98
matali.crasset@wanadoo.fr
www.matalicrasset.com
Casaderme (Pitti Imagine)
Photos: © Arrigo Coppitz
Pop Up Space (Mu.Dac)
Photos: © Corinne Cuendet
Update 3 Spaces in One: Energizer, Phytolab (Dornbracht)
Photos: © Uwe Spoering

Neil & Idle Architects (1998-2005)
Idle Architecture Studio/Christopher Idle
36 Kelso Street, Richmond 3121, Australia
P +613 9428 5202
F +613 9428 9001
info@idlearch.com.au
www.idlearch.com.au
NFORM Architects/Cameron Neil
6 Albert Street, Richmond 3121, Australia
P +613 9427 9833
F +613 9427 9844
office@n-form.com.au
www.n-form.com.au
Balmain Street Office + Studio
Photos: © Trevor Mein
Green Street Townhouses
Photos: © Rhiannon Slatter

Randy Brown Architects
1925 n. 120th Street, Omaha, NE 68154, USA
P +1 402 551 7097
F +1 402 551 2033
randy@randybrownarchitects.com
www.randybrownarchitects.com
Bizarre
Photos: © Farshid Assassi
John Luce Company
Photos: © Farshid Assassi
Modèle
Photos: © Farshid Assassi

Rice & Skinner
Level 2, 37 Swanston Street, Melbourne VIC 3000, Australia
P +613 9663 2466
F +613 9663 2477
mail@riceandskinner.com.au
www.riceandskinner.com.au
Bureau of Meteorology
Photos: © David Marks

Rudy Ricciotti
17 Boulevard Victor Hugo, 83150 Bandol, France
P +33 4 94 29 52 61
F +33 4 94 32 45 25
rudy.ricciotti@wanadoo.fr
Philharmonie
Photos: © Heike Ollertz, Philippe Ruault

Slade Architecture
150 Broadway, 807, New York, NY 10038, USA
P +1 212 677 6380
F +1 212 677 6330
info@sladearch.com
www.sladearch.com
Greenberg Van Doren Gallery
Photos: © Jordi Miralles
Miami Apartment
Photos: © Ken Hayden

Stephen Varady Architecture
14 Lackey Street (PO Box 105), St. Peters,
NSW 2044, Sydney, Australia
P +612 9516 4044
F +612 9516 4541
stephen@stephenvarady.com
www.stephenvarady.com
Larson Kelly Residence
Photos: © Stephen Varady

Studio Granda
Smidjustigur 11B, Reykjavik, IS 101, Iceland
P +354 562 2661
F +354 552 6626
studiogranda@studiogranda.is
www.studiogranda.is
Skefjar
Photos: © Sigurgeir Sigurjónsson

Takao Shiotsuka Atelier
301-4-1-24, Miyako-machi, Oita-shi, Oita 870-0034, Japan
P +81 9 7538 8828
F +81 9 7538 8829
shio-atl@shio-atl.com
www.shio-atl.com
Ohno Bus Terminal
Photos: © Kaori Ichikawa

UdA – Ufficio di Architettura
Via Valprato 68, 10155 Turin, Italy
P +39 011 248 9489
F +39 011 248 7591
uda@uda.it
www.uda.it
Ilti Luce
Photos: © Luigi Gariglio

Vidal y Asociados Arquitectos
Velázquez 78, 28001 Madrid, Spain
P +34 913 593 900
F +34 913 599 300
info@luisvidal.com
www.luisvidal.com
Restaurante Arola
Photos: © Ignacio Álvarez-Monteserín

Will Bruder Architects
111 West Monroe-Suite 444, Phoenix, AZ 85003, USA
P +1 602 324 6000
F +1 602 324 6001
willbruder@willbruder.com
www.willbruder.com
Sky Arc Residence
Photos: © Bill Timmerman

© 2007 daab
cologne london new york

published and distributed worldwide by
daab gmbh
friesenstr. 50
d - 50670 köln

p +49 - 221 - 913 927 0
f +49 - 221 - 913 927 20

mail@daab-online.com
www.daab-online.com

publisher ralf daab
rdaab@daab-online.com

creative director feyyaz
mail@feyyaz.com

editorial project by loft publications
© 2007 loft publications

editor and texts cristian campos

layout zahira rodríguez mediavilla
english translation heather bagott
german translation susanne engler
french translation michel ficerai
italian translation donatella talpo

printed in china

isbn 978 - 3 - 937718 - 60 - 6